Ninety-Five Languages
and Seven Forms of Intelligence

Studies in the
Postmodern Theory of Education

Joe L. Kincheloe and Shirley R. Steinberg
General Editors

Vol. 72

PETER LANG
New York • Washington, D.C./Baltimore • Boston • Bern
Frankfurt am Main • Brussels • Berlin • Vienna • Canterbury

D. Emily Hicks

Ninety-Five Languages and Seven Forms of Intelligence

Education in the Twenty-First Century

PETER LANG
New York • Washington, D.C./Baltimore • Boston • Bern
Frankfurt am Main • Brussels • Berlin • Vienna • Canterbury

Library of Congress Cataloging-in-Publication Data

Hicks, D. Emily.
Ninety-five languages and seven forms of intelligence: education
in the twenty-first century / D. Emily Hicks.
p. cm. — (Counterpoints; vol. 72)
Includes bibliographical references and index.
1. Critical pedagogy. 2. Postmodernism and education. 3. Multicultural
education. I. Title. II. Series: Countepoints (New York, N.Y.); vol. 72.
LC196.H53   370.11'5—dc21   97-41077
ISBN 0-8204-3909-6
ISSN 1058-1634

Die Deutsche Bibliothek-CIP-Einheitsaufnahme

Hicks, D. Emily:
Ninety-five languages and seven forms of intelligence: education
in the twenty-first century / D. Emily Hicks.
–New York; Washington, D.C./Baltimore; Boston; Bern;
Frankfurt am Main; Berlin; Brussels; Vienna; Canterbury: Lang.
(Counterpoints; Vol. 72)
ISBN 0-8204-3909-6

Cover art by D. Emily Hicks
Cover design by Nona Reuter

The paper in this book meets the guidelines for permanence and durability
of the Committee on Production Guidelines for Book Longevity
of the Council of Library Resources.

Printed in the United States of America

To my son, Guillermo Emiliano,
and in memory of his teacher and my friend, Alma Hignight

Acknowledgments

My interest in pedagogical issues and the work of Paulo Freire in particular began in 1984 at University of Southern California in a seminar in which I participated as a postdoctoral fellow in the Model Literacy Project. This interest continued in my participation in a seminar on interdisciplinary education in the humanities directed by Sylvia Wynter at San Diego State University in the late 1980s and the American Learned Societies K–12 Project in 1992–95. I am grateful to my student Alison Kreider for introducing me to the work of Joe Kincheloe and to Mexican American Studies (Chicana and Chicano Studies) for allowing me to teach a graduate seminar on the training of bilingual and bicultural teachers. The context for this research has included Grace W. Perkins Elementary School and the Barrio Logan Elementary Institute (BLEI) in San Diego, a program for first generation Mexican-American children, in which my son is participating, as well as activities involving interdisciplinary education at SDSU. Fred Lanuza, vice principal at Perkins, was an inspiration; thanks to Fred, I had the opportunity to see Freire's ideas put to the test. I also want to thank Robert Germano, director of the computer lab at Perkins, who generously gave his time to discuss pedagogical issues with me. Julio Galindo, director of BLEI, has had to face many of the challenges of multicultural education discussed in this book, and I have admired his dedication and his willingness to discuss the difficult, sometimes discouraging aspects of critical pedagogy in practice. I also want to thank all of the parents and children at Perkins and in BLEI from whom I have learned so much, especially Rosa Maria Rodriguez and Carmen Prado, and the students who participated in the binational performance, *The Kids at Perkins and Ecotina*. Beatriz Santana, my son's teacher at Perkins, has been tremendously helpful in always being available to discuss her classroom activities. Adelaida R. Del Castillo invited me to participate during 1997–8 on a committee organized to reconceptualize the university. I have been interested in Del Castillo's work since 1992, when we both were participants in a seminar at SDSU directed by Jose Limón on the culture of South Texas. She has read parts of this manuscript and she has shown infinite patience with my questions about her research. Thanks to her, I was able to bring the question of citizenship to bear upon the issues of identity, border culture, and pedagogy. The Master of Arts in Liberal Art, an interdisciplinary department at SDSU, made it possible for me to teach an interdisciplinary course, Work and Meaning, with Craig Dunn. I would like to thank Roxanne Dunbar-Ortiz for her bibliography she e-mailed me on the category of whiteness. Peter McLaren has been a source of inspiration throughout this project, and I was grateful for the opportunity to read his book, *Revolutionary Pedagogy*, as I made the final changes on the manuscript. Stanley Aronowitz and Shoji Ishitsuka generously agreed to read the entire book before it went to press. Without the patience of Tracy Eno Stearns, this book would not have been completed.

Note: An earlier version of "Nationalism, History, the Chicano Subject and the Text" was published as an occasional paper by the American Council of Learned Societies. See Emily Hicks, "Nationalism, History, the Chicano Subject and the Text," in *Teaching the Humanities: Essays from the ACLS Elementary and Secondary Schools Teacher Curriculum Development Project*, American Council of Learned Societies, ACLS Occasional Paper, No. 23, 1994. Tracy Eno Stearns and Mario T. Valdes helped edit that version, which has been expanded upon here.

Table of Contents

Preface

My own introduction to social injustice began in 1960 when I was nine years old and spent several weeks at a twelfth century Hopi village, Old Oraibi, the oldest continuously occupied town in the United States. Although the non-Hopi children had been invited by the Hopi to participate in this cultural exchange, no non-Hopi adults were allowed. The project was arranged through the San Diego Museum of Man. I slept in a schoolhouse in a sleeping bag and ate meals prepared by the Hopi P.T.A. All of the children played together inside and outside of the house. The yards were dirt, with few trees. We all played ball outside and ran in the small houses through the front doors and out the back doors. I don't remember any other toys, and there were no televisions, but we were never bored. It was always sad when my group had to return to the schoolhouse to spend the night.

My favorite memories are two: first, spending one whole afternoon sitting with a grandmother in her house while she was weaving, and second, watching the making of rolled flat bread in an outdoor stone oven, waiting for it to cook and eating it warm. I attended a snake dance, under a relentless sun, and I was amazed that no one was bitten, and no one seemed to fear the snakes. I bought two Kachina dolls, which I still have. Although I later read in our instructions, years after this experience, that we were not to take photographs during our stay, I remember that I did, and I do not remember anyone asking me not to take pictures. I collected about two dozen pottery shards, which were dated by archeologists when we returned. According to the archeologist who examined my collection, I had some twelfth century shards. I also remember that some families told us about having to drive forty miles for water. The injustice of this outraged me, and I could not understand how this could be allowed by the government.

Introduction

Critical Pedagogies and Literacies in the Borderlands

According to Cornel West, we are living at the end of the Age of Europe. It "began in 1492, with the encounter between Europeans and those who were in the new world, with the massive expulsion of the Jews in Spain" and "continued through World War II" (West 1982, 326). Situating herself as "a woman of the South," in the feminist tradition of "the politics of location" and "situated knowledges," Rosi Braidotti, in a speech on European integration, speculates about the implications of West's remark and asks if this era is not also the end of white and masculine hegemony.[1]

A notable difference between Braidotti's situation and my own is the location from which I am speaking, the U.S.-Mexico border. As Braidotti points out in the same speech, with reference to the fastest growing market in the global economy, the U.S.A.-Europe binary has given way to Asia and the Pacific Rim. The San Diego-Tijuana border finds itself in multiple global economies. It brings together the First and the Third Worlds, the U.S.A.-Europe binary and the Pacific Rim. Braidotti adds that this era is characterized by a trans-national economy and the decline of the nation state. The worker from Mexico and of Mexican descent in this region is part of the trans-national economy. In this context, I will argue that it is time for a new theory of the state and a new theory of value. What this has to do with education is best articulated by Peter McLaren in his interview with Adriana Puiggros in response to a question about whether or not there are social forces with the capacity to replace the state which could sustain the education of the majority of the population. Although McLaren is pessimistic overall, particularly about the ability of the left to act as a cohesive force in the "variety of public spheres," he notes that: "*No hay solo una esfera pública, sino múltiples . . . así hay movimientos sociales, espacios híbridos dentro de la trama cultural que presentan algunos sitios de resistencia y transformación esporádica"* (1992, 79). These multiple public spheres, hybrid spaces, which present opportunities for transformation and resistance, are the starting point for this discussion of pedagogical issues.

The hybrid spaces discussed by McLaren, and their relationship to a new theory of value, may be seen as similar to those theorized by Pirkkoliisa Ahponen, a Finnish sociologist, who has studied the cultural borders between Finland and Russia. The International Sociological Association World conference on Sociology at Montreal 1998 will include a panel entitled "Crossing Boundaries, Exceeding Alienation: Cultural Political Responses." Ahponen (1997), the panel organizer, argues that "one of the main tendencies in the development of modern society has been the institutionalization of [the] activities of citizens." She refers to this function of culture in terms of Theodor Adorno's "great denial" and the [Herbert Marcuse's] "affirmative" function of culture. As Walter Benjamin points out in his essay "Art in the Age of Mechanical Reproduction" (1969), mass culture has resulted in a democratization of culture and a loss of what he called the "aura" of the work of art. Ahponen summarizes this set of debates by noting that [ironically], the democratization of the art world, the dehierachization of cultural capital and the creation of space for popular culture and entertainment have been the "main tendencies in the institutionalization of culture." It is this complex function of culture in modern society, as both democratizing and commodified, that will be the context for a discussion of the cultural capital which has not yet been valorized in the multicultural classroom. I will ask if the price of inclusion will necessarily be commodification, just as the price of the inclusion of the non-Euroamerican child in the classroom is most often assimilation. Ahponen explains that those groups which would wish to be included in the field of cultural politics must contend with labels which imply binary oppositions. "The cultural separations between groups have been legitimized by ethnicity, gender, social class divisions and other kind[s] of ex- and inclusions" (1997). Examples of these separations in relation to multicultural capital include folk art/ high art, regional/universal, working class/middle class. Ahponen's concern is that even if democratization of culture is a growing tendency, "cultural boundaries between represented interest groups remain . . . based on . . . distinctions." These distinctions are, in Derridean terms, not only binary oppositions, but hierarchies: male/female; self/other; Euroamerican/other. She suggests that the deliberate crossing of boundaries could create a space for "a new kind of politics of culture." The international context for this discussion must be globalization and attention to the importance of knowledge as cultural capital in the information age. Specifically, I will turn my attention to the U.S.-Mexico border, which is not only a hybrid space, but the only space in the world in which the First World meets the Third World so dramatically and with such geographic precision. The cultural and economic complexity of this region at the same time may be used against these terms themselves. The state is in a period of transition, as is the notion of value. I will discuss theories of value in relation to literacies, or what McLaren refers to as *alfabetos*, in one of the following chapters. This goal of education, the acquistion of multiple literacies, is not restricted to getting a job. In fact, as I will argue in Chapter 2, the examination of border cultures may reveal that redefining democracy in border regions, and what Stanley Aronowitz and William Di Fazio (1994) call "the jobless future," will suggest aspects of a new theory of value with regard to labor. I will discuss these ideas again in Chapter 7 in relation to theoretical problems that arise when critics do not specify quite what is meant by the term "critical theory."

The roots in English departments in British colonial rule have been documented.[2] Literacy, acculturation and post-colonial relations of domination continue to be entertwined. Often, student progress in writing continues to be assessed by outmoded concepts such as numbers of spelling and grammatical errors. Howard Gardner (1985) has documented a variety of forms of intelligence. The permutations, if we are to take into account the number of linguistic groups and the different kinds of intelligence a student may possess in varying degrees, are staggering. How can alternative forms of assessment be developed, such as fluency in the variety of literacies described by McLaren, or the class solidarity established in a popular school as a measure of quality at described by Paulo Freire? In ,"Deterritorialization and Border Writing" (1988), I discuss the referential codes that must be possesed in order to understand border culture. If the teacher is not aware of these codes, he or she must learn them. The purpose of assessment needs to be questioned as well. If it is to exclude rather than to educate more effectively, then it should be abolished. I will make this argument in Chapter 5. I will also examine interdisciplinary programs and alternative forms of assessment.

What can be learned by all educators in the United States from Chicano/a, Native American and Latin American thinkers, artists and writers, well represented in the borderlands, that might be useful in classrooms throughout the United States? While the contribution to pedagogical innovations of Freire has received attention in the United States, there are many Latinas/os contributing in less well-known ways. One reason for this is the form in which they offer their critical insights. One of the most well-known, Gloria Anzaldúa (1987), writes *Borderlands* in a form that is one-half essays and one-half poetry. In order to appreciate the richness and array of contributions of Latinos/ as and Native Americans to education, we must look beyond the usual sources such as academic journal articles, conference panels and books, and to the cultural arena of mural painting, ethnic awareness groups in the elementary schools for young Latinas, novels, pow-wows, *limpias*, theatre, performance art and poetry. Of course, much of this material is not yet incorporated into the curriculum. These questions will be taken up in Chapter 1.

In this book, there is a shift in emphasis from nationalism to post-nationalism, from biculturalism to multiculturalism, from capital and labor to cultural capital and affective labor, from IQ tests and the Bell Curve to multiple forms of intelligence and assessment, and from attention to the primacy of whiteness to an interrogation of whiteness. Because these issues have an impact on the classroom from kindergarten until the student enters the workforce, this book is addressed to teachers at all levels, from K–16 to the graduate level. Chapter 1 relies on research done by high school teachers on curriculum at the high school level. The range in Chapter 3 extends from a discussion of children's literature appropriate for K–6 to works that could be taught at the university level. In Chapter 4, I discuss the magnet school concept, which operates at the K–12 level. Chapter 5, on assessment, also refers to research done on the K–12 level. The most theoretical chapters are Chapters 2, 6 and 7.

The community in which a school is located can be a resource for this information; however, teachers will have to be learners and their methods of assessment will have to change. I will address the issue of quality and assessment both in Chapter 2 and in Chapter 5. Rather than grading students individually, inspiration can be taken by teachers from Freirean Brazilian schools in which quality is measured by the sense of solidarity developed at the school.

How in educational settings as diverse and complex as those in border regions such as San Diego-Tijuana and cities such as Los Angeles is knowledge generated and legitimated? How are various border subjectivities produced in these contexts? I will address the generation of knowledge in specific non-Anglo communities in Chapter 3. One response to being part of a community whose knowledge has been historically undervalued, on the part of members of that community, is a nationalist, separatist approach to education. Departments of Chicano Studies now face the question of whether or not to merge with Ethnic Studies and/or Latin American Studies departments. What about Chicano nationalism and its role in education? If Chicano Studies merges with an umbrella that encompasses many other Latino/a identities, will the sense of Chicano identity be weakened? What deleterious effects may possibly arise from the dissolution of various department such as African American Studies, Native American Studies and Chicano Studies into Ethnic Studies? I will address these issues in Chapter 4.

How do "contact zones" continue to draw new exclusionary boundaries in the classroom? I refer to the use of the term "contact zone" found in Mary Louise Pratt's *Imperializing Eyes* (1992), in which she combines its use in linguistics and the connotative meaning of frontier zones. How can the bilingual and bicultural skills of some students be used as an asset by all students in the classroom, rather than being acculturated at the price of losing their native tongues? How can the consideration of many cultures help to break down the black/white distinction which continues to plague even the most progressive research on multiculturalism. These concerns are the focus of Chapter 2.

Asians, Native Americans, Filipinos, Chicanas and many others are neither Black nor white and Italian-Americans and Jews have become "white" fairly recently. The term "whiteness," the Nineteenth Century discussions about "whiteness" and the construction of "race" as a category can be analyzed by looking at the role of the "dark" in Spain and Latin America. While Latino students are familiar with concepts such as *la limpieza de la sangre* and the proof one's European ancestry, Anglo students are not, generally, aware of Nineteenth Century scales for measuring the amount of melanin in the hair of, for example, the Irish. In Chapter 6, I will focus on how representations of "race" appear in literature.

What problems arise when the voice of the subaltern is mediated by a European co-author, as in the case of *I, Rigoberta Menchú* (Burgos-Debray 1984)? In the work of the anthropologists, ethnologists and historians who are using multi-voiced, experimental narratives, attempts are being made by researchers to articulate their own positions as observers. The translation of the voice of the subaltern brings us to the problem of the role of intellectuals. The debates surrounding Freire's work are instructive here, both the argument against his work, and his own complex views on the role of intellectuals. Freire has been accused of, in Aronowitz's summary, "reproducing the Leninist dictum according to which the task of the avant-garde intellectuals—in this case teachers—is to lead the masses into liberation" (1994, 226). Against this view, Aronowitz focuses on Freire's call for workers, the exploited, and the oppressed to "share their power over knowledge, share the power to shape the future" (226). In Chapter 7, I attempt to put forward a model of a conceptual space where this interaction or sharing power to shape the future can occur. Freire's classrooms in Brazil do not have the cultural diversity in terms of linguistic differences of California classrooms. Aronowitz's discussion of Freire does not address the situation of the school in which over fifty languages (San Diego) or 90 languages (Los Angeles) are spoken. For this model, I turn to border cities and to the seventeenth century Dutch philosopher Baruch Spinoza, a significant figure in terms of what West calls the end of the Age of Europe due to his marginal status within that culture. West's definition of the age, intentionally or not, places the Jew in a strategic position, as he or she who cannot be assimilated, neither in 1492 in Spain nor in 1945 in Germany. Spinoza was born into a family of Sephardic Portuguese Jews; the family name was d'Espinoza. His father had been born in Portugal and had migrated to Amsterdam.[3] As a Jew in Amsterdam, Spinoza managed to outrage the Jewish community and to be "excommunicated" as a heretic. Nevertheless, he enjoyed the religious freedom of Amsterdam, a culturally diverse city that shared elements with his model of the "good" City. It is his model of the "good" City, described in his *Ethics* (1992), which I will extend to the "good" classroom. Unlike the situation in the normal city, in which urban dwellers, who do not all perceive the world the same way, and whose chance interactions are often unpleasant, in the "good" City, through the "common notion," city dwellers function together in a microcosm of an alternative form of democracy.

Notes

1. See Braidotti 1995, 1997. Braidotti refers to the ideas of "the politics of location" and "situated knowledges," which originate in the work of Adrienne Rich and Donna Haraway, respectively.

2. See Viswanathan (1989) and Delpit (1995). Viswanathan traces the roots of English as a field in colonial rule in India; Delpit discusses literacy and Australian colonial rule in Papua New Guinea.

3. See Donagan (1988). He explains Spinoza's unique situation, possible at that time only in the Netherlands, in which he was neither a member of the Jewish community nor of the Christian community, and that "[h]e was, perhaps, the first European to avow the secularization of intellectual life as an ideal, and to live it" (8).

Chapter 1

Nationalism, History, the Chicano/a Subject, and the Text

As mentioned in the introduction, I want to begin a discussion of pedagogical issues in a culturally diverse student population in a hybrid space, a border region. One of the most cohesive cultural groups in a border region is that of Chicanos/as in the U.S.-Mexico border region. To the extent that culture is language, a view that is hotly disputed in the Chicano community since many Chicanos do not speak Spanish, the Chicano community can be defined as cohesive even at the linguistic level because the border region fulfills the criteria of one type of bilingualism, described by Rosaura Sánchez (1977) as "stable bilingualism" (209). The problem for the educator in teaching not just one cultural group, but many, is that a move towards pluralism will be met with resistance by the highly developed nationalism of certain ethnic groups, particularly Chicanos/as. I want to argue that a rejection of nationalism on the part of the teacher in favor of some vague and ill-defined notion of "American democracy" is not only wrong-headed but doomed to failure in practice. I want to suggest instead that developing critical skills with students and making the notion of nationalism itself a focus of study, that is, proceeding from a comparatist approach in which students look at very different nationalist movements, is preferable to taking punitive measures with relation to Chicano nationalists by trying to silence their voices in class discussions or giving them low grades.

In the following chapter, I hope to do this by using a text that is both controversial and highly respected in the Chicano/a community, Anzaldúa's *Borderlands*, and by documenting how this book's very existence reveals that certain countervailing tendencies coexisted with heterosexuality and clearly defined gender roles even while Chicano nationalism attempted to codify and solidify Chicano/a identity. As an Anglo student pointed out to me recently, the fact that Catholicism as practiced in Mexico is shot through with pagan elements suggests that a strong reaction in the Latino community against Anzaldúa's nonconformity is hypocritical: Mexican culture itself has always refused to conform to Roman Catholicism, Spanish culture, and U.S. culture.

As Adelaida R. Del Castillo reminds us in "Introduction: Trouble and Ethnographic Endeavor," her study of gender in a lower-income neighborhood on the edge of Mexico City, even in Mexico, gender relations are not easily categorized. In her words: "[T]he cultural context of gender conflict and change, nuance and indeterminacy" can be seen as "movements from abstract, mundane and subversive levels of meaning where notions of gender do not coincide with ideal gender-based norms." In the community she studies, "this movement involves a complex interplay between ideal gender norms, actual behavior, and the strategic use of performance and pretense by Mexican men and women" (Del Castillo, n.d., n.p.).

Current events in Eastern Europe make it impossible not to be critical of nationalism, and, of course, Marxism. I begin my inquiry with the observation that until the mid-1980s, there was an antidemocratic tendency within the Chicano movement that manifested itself in the form of the suppression of alterity, specifically the otherness of the Chicana lesbian and experimental art. An analysis of this tendency will make it possible to consider a global issue, the relationship between democracy and alterity. I propose that one way to test the premise expressed by Jürgen Habermas (1985) and others, that modernism is based on the integration rather than the exclusion of alterity, is to turn to the work of spokespersons of alterity, Chicana lesbians.[1] To the extent that they have been included, might conclude that Habermas is correct. On the other hand, it could also be argued that it is because we are now in a postmodern era that there is a space for the work of Chicana lesbians.[2] In addition to the work of Marie Collins and Sue Anderson (1993, 1992–1995), my methodological approach in this essay draws on work done in cultural studies and particularly of multicultural art, such as Lucy R. Lippard's *Mixed Blessings.* (1990)[3] I will argue that Friedrich Nietzsche's concept of the Dionysian has been repressed in Chicano nationalist and Marxist culture. The link between the Dionysian and alterity in the context of democracy has been developed by Antonio Negri and Michael Hardt (1994). In a lecture at the University of California, San Diego, the Chicano poet Alurista characterized Chicano literature as falling into three phases: (1) The Nascent Period (1965–75); (2) The Assimilationist Period (1975–85); and (3) The Current Period (1985–present). In the first phase, basic social tension was largely related to racial and cultural issues. In the second, class distinctions were dominant. in the third and present period, conflicts over gender issues dominate. I will use Alurista's categories as markers if not guideposts. They will prove to be both useful but, if applied too rigidly, ultimately inadequate; Chicana writing did not just emerge; it has existed all along. Only sexism can be the sufficient, if not the necessary, explanation for the exclusion of the discussion of gender issues in the first two periods.

The use I am making of Friedrich Nietzsche's categories *Apollonian* and *Dionysian* is merely a starting point to get back to the moment of the theft or appropriation of the feminine, in both Western theatre and pre-Colombian cultures. It would be more accurate to speak of the pre-Apollonian/Dionysian, or perhaps of the time to which Gloria Anzaldúa refers in *Borderlands*, a time before the division of the various attributes of Coatlicue into "good" and "evil."[4] It is the assimilation of female sexuality and Dionysus that makes the discussion so complex. By analogy the Virgin of Guadalupe may be seen as linked to conservative political forces, as she is in Mexico in the *guadalupana* movement, or as a many-layered icon who ultimately harkens back to Tonantsín, as she is seen by Anzaldúa and many Chicanas. Similarly, Dionysus, Nietzsche's appropriation of Dionysus, and the notion of "becoming-woman" may be rejected by some feminists on the grounds that men are usurping the feminine.[5] Conversely, the Dionysian can be reclaimed in order to ground it in an older pantheon of female deities, as I am attempting to do in this discussion.

Three passages which deal with modernity, history, and capitalism have captured my attention lately, and I have returned to them compulsively. I believe they contextualize the problems of nationalism and the subject and allow us to enter into the arena of the relationship between democracy and alterity. The first, which refers to the views of French philosopher Michel Foucault, comes from Luc Ferry and Alan Renaut's *French Philosophy of the Sixties.*

Contrary to Foucault's claim, the dynamics of modernity are not essentially that of the exclusion of otherness. The logic of modern societies is rather more like the one Tocqueville describes, namely, the logic of integration sustained by the proposition of the fundamental equality of all man[sic]kind (1990, 90).

I consider this view to be Habermasian. It could be argued that modernity excludes otherness precisely by integrating and assimilating it until it is no longer recognizable as alterity. I find that Anzaldúa's documentation of the exclusion of otherness in the borderlands refutes this statement. Jürgen Habermas's optimism regarding the "dignity of modernity" and the possibility of a dialogue, in which all parties would be able to begin and end the conversation and give and receive orders, fails to recognize the very real concerns about dialogue addressed by Anzaldúa.[6] In which language would the dialogue occur? Anzaldúa lists eight "languages" she speaks, all related to Spanish and/or English, that are found in the U.S.-Mexico region alone. The treatment of the other, poignantly portrayed in such poems as "We Call Them Greasers," hardly speaks to modernism's ablity to integrate the other.

The second, from Fredric Jameson in *The Political Unconscious*, appears in the context of commentary on Louis Althusser's antiteleological formula for history, and its relation to Jacques Lacan's notion of the Real and Spinoza's idea of the "absent cause":

> [I]t [the real] is inaccessible to us except in textual form . . . as an absent cause, [it] necessarily passes through its prior textualization, its narrativization in the political unconsciousness (1985, 35).

Both passages raise issues which would have to be part of an inquiry into the nature of the logic of modern society from the perspective of someone living in the borderlands and which would help us to formulate various alternative viewpoints regarding the relationship between democracy and alterity. Whether or not the logic of modern society is based on the exclusion of otherness or the logic of integration, and whether or not we can only know history in textual form, would have to be part of an inquiry into the nature of the logic of modern society. One version of this might go as follows: If we can only know history in textual form, then in order to answer the question about whether or not the logic of modern society is based on the exclusion of otherness, we might want to turn to literary texts about the exclusion of otherness. Certainly, the work of contemporary Chicana lesbian writers is useful here, as is the research of Collins and Anderson and their use of the notion of "the generational unit," in order to study the history of the Chicano movement and one of its central figures, Luis Valdez.

Finally, because a theory of the voice of the subaltern may itself be merely a contemporary form of colonialism, it is useful here to consider Gayatri Spivak. She argues, in "Can the Subaltern Speak?," that Deleuze and Foucault's insistence on the subaltern's ability to speak (1977) is comparable to British attempts to outlaw widow suicide in India: "[I]t is another case of white men telling brown men what to do with brown women" (Spivak 1988, 305).[7] Nevertheless, in the following passage, she accurately explains their model:

> Their suggestion, summarized, is that, since capital decodes and deterritorializes the socius by releasing the abstract [cf. Nietzsche's slave logic] as such, capitalism manages the crisis by way of the generalized psycho-analytic mode of production of affective value, which operates via a generalized system of affective equivalence, however spectacular in its complexity and discontinuity (Spivak 1993, 91; brackets added).

Although this may have not been intentional, Spivak's reference to affect can alert the reader to Spinoza and his discussion of affect in the *Ethics*. Spinoza's theory of affects would take us beyond the confines of this paper. Suffice it to say that Spivak is discussing the links that connect us through desire and how, according to Deleuze and Guattari, capitalism manages and controls these connections by reducing their differences to "a system of affective equivalence." McLaren's notion of *alfabetismos* and the necessity of learning to become literate in multiple *alfabetismos* is relevant here in that our desire is managed by *alfabetismos*. (McLaren 1992, 78–81). Spinoza's theory of affects is discussed by the Italian critic Negri in relation to his conception of social organization and liberation grounded not in capitalism but an alternative tradition of democracy, making Spinoza a "savage anomaly." In Spinoza's "good" City inhabitants would have the opportunity to encounter each other by chance, which, rather than being unpleasant, might led to joyful interaction. In the next chapter, I will extend these ideas to the "good" classroom. Spinoza's model allows for the inclusion of alterity without the homogenization of difference. Deleuze argues that there is a tradition of thought that runs from Spinoza to Nietzsche that does not lead to Hegel's dialectic and the subsumption of difference. How to bring the voices of the excluded into a discussion of history is what finally brings us back to the cultural production of Chicana lesbian writers and their emergence in this historic moment, that is to the beginning of this essay. The following pages describe the emergence of an audience for Chicana writing against the background of the activist theatre of Valdez and others, and while doing so, engages in a discussion of the issues of the adequacy of periodization to account for the development of an audience for Chicana writing.

If we shift from a theoretical discussion of democracy and alterity to the concreteness of the classroom using Jean-Paul Sartre as a model, with the reminder that he taught in the *lycée*, there should be nothing unusual about referring to the research of two high school teachers in the United States. Recently Sue Anderson and Marie Collins, who both teach in high schools, asked me how I would teach Anzaldúa's work, particularly to their Latino/a high school students, given the homophobia the teachers knew they would face. I had been impressed with their attempts to bring Chicano/a culture into the high school curriculum in their joint research project entitled "Affirmation, Resistance, Transformation" (1993). They explained that they had not included Anzaldúa in the curriculum yet, but they wanted to do so; furthermore, they had been influenced by her work. In their curriculum project "Team-Based Curriculum: The Emergence of the Chicano," (1992–1995) they look at the 1960s and 1970s from Chicano/a perspectives, while grappling with both historical and pedagogical issues and discussing three alternative pedagogies: constructivism, critical pedagogy, and feminist pedagogy. They use the concept of the "historical generation" to frame their work. I believe they have made a significant contribution to gender studies with their project, and I am presenting my own research in relation to theirs. Their work may shed some light on the Habermas-Deleuze debates with which I begin this essay.[8]

Collins and Anderson create a curriculum "which allows the teacher to continue to teach the 'major' events of the traditional canon of American history" but point out that "the concept of generational units allows the flexibility to examine the response of various cultural groups as well as gender and class groups (1993, 4). I found this concept to be very compatible with Deleuze and Guattari's notion of "minor" or what I would call "border" culture and, furthermore, an appropriate context for Anzaldúa's work. A generation may not be biologically or geographically homogeneous; rather, its members can be linked politically and form a collective voice, although their voices are not identical (Deleuze and Guattari 1986, 16–27). While living between cultures, they react to a set of shared experiences, as do Anglos and Latinos living in the U.S.-Mexico border region. Collins and Anderson refer to Marvin Rintale's definition of generation: "a group of human beings who have undergone the same historical experiences" (1993, 4). The shared historical experiences Anderson and Collins discuss include membership in the "baby boom" generation;

McCarthyism; the Berlin Wall and the Cuban Missile Crisis, detente; nationalist movements in Cuba, Bangladesh, and African nations; Vietnam; political assassinations, in the United States; Watts; and Watergate. The responses to these experiences covered in their curriculum include the black Civil Rights Movement, the Students' Youth Movement, Women's Liberation, the Chicano Movement, the American Indian Movement, and the War on Poverty. In thinking about shared historical experiences, I found it useful to return to the work of Ernst Bloch, "Nonsynchrony and its Obligation to Dialectics" (1977). Bloch argues that we do not all experience a given historical period the same way. For example, not everyone experienced 1968 the same way in which many French students, workers and intellectuals did (Bloch 1977, 22–38). Anderson and Collins underscore the importance of highlighting "difference within difference" in their discussion of the 1960s. Although they do not yet include Anzaldúa and Cherríe Moraga in their curriculum, they have laid the groundwork for doing so: the Chicana lesbian is the quintessential example of "difference within difference." It is in the context of their emphasis on alterity that I can introduce Nietzsche's categories.

I would argue that the Dionysian allows for alterity and that the Apollonian dominated the Dionysian in the early days of Chicano theatre, but that the tension between cultural nationalists and marxists reveals that the Dionysian/Coatlicuan conflict with the Apollonian was present. That is, there was a space for the Dionysian among some cultural nationalists, particularly in relation to pre-Conquest culture, a space that did not interest most Marxists. Nevertheless, it is not until recently, in the work of the "new generation" of Chicana writers, that the Dionysian has been allowed to emerge. I hope to uncover some of the rhizomatic relationships that connect form and content, "the traditional" and the experimental, and the Dionysian and the Apollonian in relation to contemporary Chicana writing. The contribution of conceptual art to the encouragement of formal experimentation among Chicana writers, and the demise of both Chicano nationalism and Marxism have coincided with the outpouring of literary production from and audience support for Chicana writers. Despite the limitations placed on gender definition imposed by the historical antecedents of Chicano/theatre, including *commedia dell'arte, carpa*, and morality plays, and the forms favored by Valdez, the *acto*, the *mito*, and the *corrido*, new genres and reworking of older genre have emerged to allow for new forms of gender definition in theatre. This "new generation" connects women of different ages and sexual preferences, spanning twenty years. Whereas some of the younger writers are getting recognition in their twenties, their older sisters are getting the recognition they deserve in their forties. To make the point as strongly as possible, my premise is that Moraga's work is not only more relevant than Valdez's, but it has been for the last fifteen years, more useful in considering democracy and its relation to alterity.

Moraga has written about sexism in the Chicano movement in *Loving in the War Years* (1983). Regarding the early period, during which youth and students of the Chicano movement developed a separatist, cultural nationalist philosophy, Collins and Anderson describe "the utopian '*El plan espiritual de Aztlán*,'" adopted in March 1969 at a conference in Denver, Colorado: "it called for the reclamation and control of lands stolen from Mexico (the U.S. Southwest), anti-Europeanism, an insistence on the importance and glory of brown-skinned Indian heritage and an emphasis on humanistic and non-materialistic culture and education" (1993). This important document did not address gender issues.

The situation is further complicated by the splitting described by Anzaldúa: "The male-dominated Azteca-Mexica culture drove the powerful female deities underground by giving them monstrous attributes and by substituting male deities in their place, by splitting the female Self and the female deities" (1987, 27). I cannot overemphasize this point.

The most overtly political and didactic form used by Valdez was the *acto*; not surprisingly, it is somewhat limited both in terms of its depth of analysis of feminist issues and its openness to experimental elements. The common drudgery and difficulties suffered by men in low-paying jobs and housewives were presented in parallel. In defense of the *acto*, Jorge Huerta (1982) notes that the high cost of living, unemployment, and inadequate housing made early Chicano theatre closer to the *acto* than to Ibsen. More contemporary Chicana feminists go further than both the *acto* and Ibsen: Anzaldúa and Moraga write about deeper spiritual, sexual, and creative processes in women. The problem with the early *actos* is that the daily conflicts that become their scenarios all had one solution in common: "Join the union." Unfortunately, joining the union was not an adequate solution to gender issues. The union does not appear in Moraga's plays "Giving up the Ghost" (1983) and "Shadow of a Man" (1992).

Unlike the *acto*, the *mito* is a form more amenable to a serious treatment of gender issues. Huerta writes: "To Valdez, the *acto* portrays the Chicano through the eyes of man, while the *mito* sees the Chicano through the eyes of God" (Huerta 1992, 97). Note that neither see through the eyes of the Chicano; nevertheless, the spirituality in the *mito* brings us closer to the Dionysian/Coatlicuan.

The *corrido* is another prominent form in Valdez's work; unlike the *acto* and *mito*, it forms an integral part of Mexican culture. Just as the musical form of the *cumbia* embraced the issue of AIDS in Tijuana in the mid-1980s, there could conceivably be feminist *corridos* in the future. Collins and Anderson have students write their own *corridos*.

Having looked at three major elements in Valdez's work, the *acto*, the *mito*, and the *corrido*, I now want to address briefly the influence on Valdez's work of such figures as Bertholt Brecht. Following Brecht, Valdez has privileged a didactic approach to theatre. Nondidactic forms were rejected by *El teatro campesino* because some *campesinos* said they could not understand them.

What experimental currents existed alongside of, although perhaps out of sight from, Chicano *teatro*? Moraga began writing *Loving in the War Years* in 1976. As Moraga explains, her sense of Chicana identity grew out of her growing sense of lesbian identity. Given the attitudes about homosexuality that were prevalent in the Chicano movement during the 1970s, this is not surprising. Nor is it surprising that she found alternative forms in which to write, which did not include the *acto* or the *mito*; none of Valdez's work to date has addressed the situation of the lesbian Chicana.

We can return to *commedia dell'arte*, *carpa*, and morality plays to continue to explore the construction of gender in various theatrical forms that have influenced Chicano theatre. The multiplicity of forms found in *carpa*, which includes vignettes, songs, and dances, forms linked mainly by the fact that they could be performed under a tent by a traveling troupe, make *carpa* a genre that is conducive to the discussion of contemporary issues, including gender issues. Like the "slices of life" in the PBS production of Valdez's "*Corridos*," "slices of life" continue to be part of the work of contemporary Chicana lesbian comedians/performance artists such as Monica Palacios and Marga Gómez. Both Palacios and Gómez use humor to explore gender issues. "A Slice of Life" and the telling of stories are also combined in the work of the Native American performance group Spiderwoman Theatre.

The prescriptive attitudes toward gender roles in morality plays make this a rich form for reworking in a contemporary context. although written during The Nascent Period (in 1973), in *El Jardín*,

Carlos Morton (1983) does look at gender in a provocative manner. Huerta explains that "the premise of the play is 'What if Adam and Eve were Chicanos and God a rich early Californian'" (1982, 196)? What remains intriguing about the play is the way in which the relation between a man and a woman is negotiated in the context of racism and the Church. When performed by Diana Contreras in 1992 at the Centro Cultural de la Raza in San Diego, the strength and eroticism of Eve was strikingly contemporary and closer to Chicana lesbian writers in its interrogation of gender construction; it did not merely reiterate a simple virgin/whore dichotomy.

The urgency of the United Farm Workers situation in the late 1960s, the influences of Marxism and Chicano nationalism, and the lack of recognition of gender construction as a crucial part of political analysis resulted in a truncated Dionysian/Coatlicuan in Chicano theatre of the Nascent Period. In other words, there was a suppression of alterity within the Chicano movement. For example, in San Juan Bautista, Chicanos dressed for the Day of the Dead celebrations, using images that evoked the carnivalesque, in Mikhail Bakhtin's sense, and the Dionysian, in Nietzsche's sense. The context for these images however, was Apollonian; it was the use of theatre to teach and to politicize. The didactic overpowered the Dionysian. It was not until Chicana feminism and conceptual art on the West Coast, from the Bay Area to Mexico City, entering from Brazil, not just Europe, freeing the Latino/ a artist from Western logic and European neocolonialism, that a force as visually strong as the didactic art of Chicano murals and early *teatro campesino* could successfully counter these forms. We can compare the Day of the Dead celebration of the Nascent period, in which gay and lesbian identity was not addressed, to the Day of the Dead Celebration in San Francisco in 1986, for example, when the gay and lesbian communities joined forces with Chicanos in the Mission District to create a parade of stunningly beautiful floats containing altars memorializing those who had died of AIDS.

It was only after the convergence of "folk ritual" and the "secret history of women" as it informed the work of women linked to both overtly political and conceptual art that the Dionysian could again be freed in the work of Latinas such as *altarista* and critic Amalia Mesa-Bains. As Ramón Saldívar writes in *Chicano Narrative*:

> [N]o study of Chicano narrative . . . would be complete without a consideration of the most vibrant new development in Chicano literature, the emer-

gence of a significant body of works by women authors in the 1970s and 1980s (1990, 172).

He adds, "Chicana writers are . . . building an instructive alternative to the exclusively phallocentric subject of contemporary Chicano narrative" (Saldívar 1990, 175).

In conclusion, feminist pedagogy and gender studies can play an important role at the high school level; conversely, research generated in the classroom can be illuminating in the context of current debates in gender studies and in the global discussion of democracy, our understanding of modern societies, and the analysis of capital logic. In "After Aztlán . . . a New Generation of Latino Writers," the final lesson of Collins and Anderson's curriculum, students read Cisneros, Latina/o poets of the nineties, and other contemporary work. They are encouraged to meet muralist Judy Baca and to visit the art gallery and community center Self-help Graphics. The research of Collins and Anderson, particularly the use of the notion of "generational unit," is preparing the way for the creation of a curriculum in which the work of contemporary Chicana writers can be understood. With the fracturing of the paradigms of cultural nationalism and Marxism in the border region, Chicanas find themselves relating to Aztec culture and to Aztlán in a new way. While developed in the high schools, the project of Collins and Anderson will have far-reaching implications for the teaching of Chicana writers at the university level. Their work can contextualize the introduction of Chicana lesbian writers at the university, one hopes, at the high school level. Their research is being carried out, not insignificantly, on the West Coast, which can no longer be seen only in relation to the East Coast, or even to the north/south division between the United States and Mexico, but instead as part of a Pacific Rim recentering. As such, it opens up new ways of thinking about how cultural groups may function in relation to one another in a multicultural classroom. The rejection of cultural nationalism by contemporary Chicana writers may serve as a paradigm for different rhizomatic connections linking culture, nation, and gender in other border regions. It is a call for the necessity to go beyond both a cultural nationalist politics and aesthetics. It is an opportunity to reconsider the relationship between democracy and alterity.

Notes

1. This formulation of the relationship between modernity and alterity Habermasian formulation. In his *Introduction to Observations on "The Spiritual Situation of the Age"* (1985), Habermas distinguishes himself from the New Right: "The New Right warns against the discursive dissolution of values, against the erosion of natural traditions, against the overburdening of the individual, and against excessive individualism. Its adherents want to see modernization restricted to capitalist growth and technical progress while at the same time wishing to arrest cultural transformation, identity formation, changes in motivation and attitude—in short, to freeze the contents of tradition. By contrast we must again bring to consciousness the dignity of modernity, the dimension of a non-truncated rationality" (15). Habermas is also the author of *Knowledge and Human Interests*.

2. Shoji Ishitsuka (1996) makes a link between the attention to gender and postmodernism. In "Nietzsche and Performance" (1996), I develop my view that the postmodernist era has been more hospitable to Chicana and Chicana lesbian culture than was the modernist era.

3. Anderson and Collins are Los Angeles area high school teachers. They both participated as post-secondary fellows in 1992–93 in the UCLA workshop of the ACLS Program in Humanities Curriculum Development.

4. As Anzaldúa explains in *Borderlands*, the female deities were driven underground by Azteca-Mexica culture:
   "[T]hey divided her who had been complete, who possessed both upper (light) and underworld (dark) aspects. Coatlicue, the Serpent goddess, and her more sinister aspects, Tlazolteotl and Cihuacoatl were 'darkened' and disempowered much in the same manner as the Indian Kali" (1987, 27).

5. Spivak's attack on the concept of "becoming woman" can be found in "Can the Subaltern Speak?" (1988, 308).

6. Habermas addresses the problem of modernity in these terms in his introduction to *Observations on "The Spiritual Situation of the Age"* (1985). Seyla Benhabib has written about the ideal speech situation in her essay "The Utopian Dimension in Communicative Ethics" (1992).

7. I want to thank Jim Merod for bring it to my attention at the Conference on Postmodern Culture at National University, Diego (1992) that Spivak adopted a more pro-Foucault position after the publication of "Can the Subaltern Speak?"

8. In my essay "Foucault's Ventriloquism" (1995), I address both the Habermas-Deleuze debates and Spivak's attack on Foucault and Deleuze.

Chapter 2

Boundaries in the Classroom: Teacher-Student "Contact Zones" and Spinoza's "Good" Classroom

Nationally, multiculturalism and postmodernism are two movements which have created a context in that classroom boundaries are being defined theoretically; in states such as California, demographic shifts have created a context in which new linguistic, ethnic, religious, cultural, and class boundaries are being defined in practice. At the same time, legislation stigmatizing the Other has come in many forms, including the English Only movement, Proposition 187, Proposition 209 and the dismantling of affirmative action; these forms of stigmatizing the Other are occurring in what Antonio Gramsci calls political society and civil society, that is, in both the legal realm and in educational institutions. The discourses of orthodox marxism and French, American (Anglo) and British (English) feminism have not been adequate to address these issues; to further complicate matters, some feminists, including some Chicana feminists and African-American feminists have been critical of some forms of feminism and some tenets of postmodernism. A Chicana feminist whose work on border culture and border subjectivity is crucial in the discussion of multiculturalism is Gloria Anzaldúa. In "Deterritorialization and Border Writing" (1988), I argue that in order to understand border literature, the reader has to learn the referential codes of the border subject. The notion of the border in relation to teaching is also taken up by Giroux in his essay "Border Pedagogy in the Age of Postmodernism," in *Postmodern Education*, in which he writes: "Border pedagogy offers the opportunity for students to engage the multiple references that constitute different cultural codes, experiences and languages" (1990, 118–19). Of great relevance to the discussion of the teaching of different cultural codes are McLaren's (1992) notions of multiple public spheres, including hybrid spheres, and multiple literacies. One of the literacies McLaren emphasizes is media literacy. The acquisition of multiple literacies, as articulated by McLaren, is an extension of Paolo Freire's work insofar as it depends on an interaction between teacher and student in which there may be a reversal of roles. In this model, both teacher and student must acquire multiple literacies. In this chapter, I will (1) put forward a model of a "good" multicultural classroom; (2) discuss the teaching of multiple literacies, the acknowledging of multiple perspectives and the ways in which the "good" classroom provides a context for a curriculum based on these literacies and perspectives; (3) refer to current debates in literary theory regarding language, postmodernism and multiculturalism; and (4) address attacks on affirmative action and bilingual education, including the English Only movement.

As Joe Kincheloe points out in *Towards a Critical Politics of Teacher Thinking*, the advent of scientific modernism is grounded in the philosophies of René Descartes, Isaac Newton, and Francis Bacon: "The world is rational (logocentric) and there is only one meaning of the term" (1993, 3). While postmodernists and advocates of multiculturalism have focused their attacks on Cartesian rationality, often citing Michel Foucault and Deleuze, both of whom were influenced by Baruch Spinoza, Spinoza's work has not received the same attention in pedagogical debates. Spinoza gives us an alternative form of rationality, one that takes our affects into account, and, like Freire, he is committed to a democratic restructuring of society. As Gramsci tells us in "On Education":

> [D]emocracy, by definition, cannot mean merely that an unskilled worker can become skilled. It must mean that every "citizen" can "govern" and that society places him, even if only abstractly, in a position to do this. Politically democracy tends toward a coincidence of the rulers and ruled (in the sense of government with the concept of the governed) (1992, 40).

We will see how Negri, reading Spinoza, generates a similar definition of democracy.

Gramsci's notion of hegemony is useful in understanding the forces that mitigate against the acquisition of multiple literacies as well as the interstices in which this learning can take place. Gramsci's complex and shifting distinction between political and civil society is important in conceptualizing the relationship between this model of the classroom and the state. I will look at civil society in Spinoza's discussion of the "good" City. Negri's persuasive analysis of Spinoza as providing an alternative view of democracy makes the work of this seventeenth century philosopher relevant in the contemporary postmodern era; furthermore, precisely because in postmodern society the Third World exists within the First World in large cities, I find Spinoza's description of the "good" City to be very suggestive. The border city is a hybrid sphere that functions as one of the multiple public spheres described by McLaren.

Deleuze explains in *Expressionism in Philosophy* that for Spinoza, there can only be one way of making the state of nature viable. In order to protect oneself from chance encounters, which may be unpleasant, the alternative is to organize the encounters. (261) Deleuze writes:

> As long as [humans] live by chance encounters, as long as they are affected by chance passions, men are led in various directions and so have no chance of meeting in relations that agree: they are opposed to one another. We can, it is true, avoid this conflict to the extent that we bring into play a very slow learning process, a very slow empirical education (1992, 265).

This slow process can last a lifetime, but it can hastened by residence in the State or City (Deleuze 1992, 265). Spinoza's state is not a Hobbesian state, in which "a third party . . . gains by the contract made by individuals," ruled by a sovereign "defined by his natural right, equal to his power, equal, that is, to all the rights relinquished by the contracting parties" (266). Rather, "Spinoza describes the City as a collective person, with common body and soul, 'a multitude which is guided, as it were, by one mind'" (1992, 266). In thinking about this City in relation to border culture, I am reminded of Deleuze and Guattari's *Kafka* (1986), in which one of the characteristics of minor literature is that it is collective. Although Deleuze does not discuss the deterritorialized subject in *Expressionism in Philosophy*, suggestive parallels may be drawn between "the multitude" discussed by Spinoza and emphasized by Deleuze, and "the collective." Of course, in Spinoza's time, there was a great imbalance between the Power (*potestas*) of the State and the power (*potentia*) of the multitude.[1]

Foucault's analysis of power as both oppressive and productive will form an important part of the model. To paraphrase Spinoza, to exist in the borderlands is to have power in the borderlands; another aspect of power, in addition to existence, is the power to be affected. The border dweller has access to at least a double set of referential codes, which increases the power to be affected. Using two images, first, of Mary Louise Pratt's (1992) contact zone, and second, of Spinoza's "good" City, I will put forward a model of a multicultural classroom in postmodernist culture in which the acquisition of multiple literacies for all students and teachers could theoretically occur. Because I will focus on the Latino community in the U.S.-Mexico border region, I find Pratt's contact zone to be appropriate. As Timothy Dunn argues in *The Militarization of the Border* (1996), the Chicano community can be seen as a colonized community; Pratt developed her model in relation to the contact/conquest that links the Old and the New World. The border dweller has access to at least a double set of referential codes, which increases the power to be affected.

I want to examine the multicultural classroom as it exists and as it could exist in postmodern culture. I will use Freire's ideas about pedagogy as a starting point for analyzing this classroom, as Stanley Aronowitz describes them, as: "a system in which the locus of the learning process is shifted from the teacher to the student" (1994, 219). Although Freire's students are Brazilian *campesinos*, his methods are relevant to the multicultural classroom in the United States. As Aronowitz explains, Freire believes education to be a space in which students can "'develop their power to perceive critically the way they exist in the world'" (Aronowitz 1994, 222, quoting Freire 1990, 71. Emphasis in original.). Kincheloe writes in *Toward a Critical Politics of Teaching Thinking, Mapping the Postmodern*:

> Marilyn Ferguson uses the multicultural image of the Cheyenne Wheel of Knowledge to conceptualize . . . [a] . . . higher dimension of human experience, the realm of human becoming . . . [T]he Cheyenne developed a system of meaning to help them make sense of the world and their relationship to it. Thus, in the spirit of the Cheyenne we learn to think in a way that allows us to make sense of our place on the planet, our role in the pageant of history, our connection to the quantum world of the subatomic and the immensity of the universe, and of our relationship to birth, death, work, and family without an appreciation of implicate systems and the way the unfolding affects us, we are lost in the cosmos, incapable of transcending the formal cognition of modernist reductionism. Without our postmodern wheel of knowledge, we find "being" easier than "becoming" (1993, 104).

The Cheyenne Wheel of Knowledge suggests a cosmology, as do the Quabbalah and the cosmologies of Afro-Cuban religions. For the nonwhite, nonmiddle-class student, the classroom can become a place in which to make sense of one's place on the planet. For the white, middle-class student, the classroom can become a place in which to understand the privilege of one's place on the planet. To this I want to add Anzaldúa's Coatlicue state and Spinoza's "good" City as parts of a heuristic device for conceptualizing a multicultural classroom in which all students could have the opportunity to learn. This model does not pretend to be universal; it merely provides a way to raise important issues about the multicultural classroom. One certainty about the multicultural classroom of the future is that it will not have to be based on the Anglo middle-class values described by McLaren in *Life in Schools* (1989). Class may begin a few minutes late; however, students may stay in class during the break and continue talking to each other after the class. McLaren writes about the "cultural capital of the dominant culture" which teachers often define as being related to completed homework, punctuality, politeness, unobtrusiveness and deference to authority, behavior which some students associate with "acting white" (1989, 211–212). In the good classroom of the future, the Internet may make these behaviors irrelevant. Hopefully, a respect for more than one cultural code will place an emphasis on the power relations in which these behaviors are embedded. I will discuss the concept of cultural capital in greater detail in Chapter Five, "Culture, Narrativity, and Assessment."

While just perceiving critically one's position in the world could limit the student to an individual educational path, Spinoza's alternative model of democracy, as articulated by Negri, suggests a revolutionary process. Negri writes in *The Savage Anomaly*: "The only truth that Spinoza accepts from his times and maintains in its purity" is the "pressure toward a revolutionary reconstruction of the world" (1991, 180). It is the "link between knowledge and power through self-directed action" that characterizes Freire's pedagogy (223). In Spinoza's model, this link, found in the common notion, can arise in a multicultural environment in which, as Spinoza expresses it in the *Ethics* (1677, 1992), not all men [sic] see the same object the same way. I will argue that this link cannot be abstract ideas. Nietzsche reveals the inadequacy of universal notions in his essay "On Truth and Lies in a Nonmoral Sense." For Spinoza, abstract ideas, based on sensible differential characteristics, are inadequate because sensible characteristics are extremely variable. The common notions are neither transcendental terms nor universal notions (Deleuze 1992, 277). It is through reason, but not Cartesian reason, that human beings will be guided to live in harmony with others. Negri (1991, 165–66) quotes Spinoza from the *Ethics*: "'He who lives according to the guidance of reason strives, as far as he can, to repay the other's Hate, Anger, and Disdain toward him, with love, or Generosity' (Proposition 46) At the practical level on the playground, this must be translated into conflict resolution supported by a well-staffed counseling center and a faculty and staff with a shared vision about a multicultural future.

I have chosen Anzaldúa's Coatlicue state as a way to conceptualize the journey from blocked, negative emotions because it allows us to discuss affects in border culture. In *Borderlands*, she explains the Coatlicue state as a journey from shame through addiction. Before her journey, she is paralyzed by shame, a shame rooted her social class, her ways of speaking Spanish, the color of her skin, and her gender preference. "Held in thrall" by one's addiction, action is impossible (Anzaldúa 1987, 45). The refusal to deal with the addiction brings on the Coatlicue, which includes a descent into *miktlan*, the underworld. Here, she confronts Coatlicue, a pre-Colombian goddess with no head or hands; in the place of a head are twin rattlesnakes. "Hanging from her neck is a necklace of open hands alternating with human hearts" (47). The Coatlicue state, which includes a confrontation with this goddess, who brings together opposites, is a prelude to crossing over to a state of consciousness in which shame and fear are overcome and action is possible. For the nonwhite child, shame can make the process of learning much more difficult. Anzaldúa's embracing of her culture suggests a way for teachers to embrace the cultures of their students; her journey suggests a way for teachers to make their own descents into *miktlan*.

Spinoza also believes that action is made impossible when negative emotions paralyze the subject. Spinoza delineates two sets of distinctions: (1) sad vs. joyful passions; and (2) passions and actions. Although joyful passions give us more power, we will "remain passive, separated from our power," until we have an adequate rather than a confused idea of an affecting body and "these active joys . . . no longer imply transitions and passages . . ." (Deleuze 1988, 51). It is only by a "genuine 'leap,'" that we understand, act, and are reasonable (Deleuze 1992, 283). Although Spinoza writes about the subject in civil society, we can extend his analysis of the affects to the multicultural classroom.

While in Anzaldúa's discussion of the Coatlicue state as a prelude to crossing, the border subject's descent and confrontation with

Coatlicue takes place in solitude, in Spinoza's discussion of the relationship between affects and action, the transition from passivity to action takes place most efficiently in the city. In the model I am putting forward, I want to place the border subject in the border city. As described by Deleuze, Spinoza's "good" City

> both takes the place of reason for those who have none, and prepares, prefigures and its way imitates the work of reason. It is the City that makes possible the development of reason itself. One should not take as signs of excessive optimism Spinoza's two propositions that, everything considered, the City is the best environment in which man can become reasonable, and that it is also the best environment in which a reasonable man [sic] can live (1992, 268).

Spinoza's reason, unlike Descartes's, is not based on a mind-body split; furthermore, it is linked to freedom. While the citizen in Spinoza's "good" City renounces rights personally, he or she preserves them in the civil state. Deleuze explains that for Spinoza, "the power of knowing, thinking and expressing one's thought remains an inalienable natural right . . . " (1992, 267). For Spinoza, "nobody is born reasonable" and "[n]obody is born a citizen" (259). What makes this interesting from a border perspective is that it calls into question the notion of citizenship. It suggests, as does Adelaida R. Del Castillo, that a border dweller who has become "reasonable" by virtue of being situated on cultural, linguistic, economic and other borders is a "citizen" because he or she participates, reasonably, in a community, regardless of country of birth. The implications for the classroom include the understanding that it is not enough for the nonwhite student to be allowed to think differently from the Anglo norm; all students should be able to express themselves as well. Spinoza's view of consent is relevant to discipline in the classroom: "The principle of consent (pact or contract) becomes the principle of political philosophy, and replaces the rule of authority" (260). In an explanatory note to the chapter of *Expressionism in Philosophy* entitled "The Ethical Vision of the World," Deleuze writes, referring to Spinoza's *Political Treatise*: "The City, once established, must elicit the love of freedom rather than the fear of punishments or even the hope of rewards. [As Spinoza writes], 'Rewards of virtue are granted to slaves, not freemen' (391, note 33). If we apply this to the classroom, we can see that in the good classroom, the love of freedom, not the fear or punishment or the hope of rewards would motivate students. To encourage this, teachers would not be obsessed with punitive grading systems but rather, in accordance with Freire's goal, with creating a politically conscious school environment. I propose that teachers and students in border cities have a unique opportunity in which to make this attempt. Border cities are not only those which link two countries, but also those in which inhabitants of a variety of cultural, ethnic and linguistic backgrounds meet. Because border cities bring together inhabitants from a variety of backgrounds, border subjects are capable of being affected in a great many ways, that is, at least twice as many ways as monocultural subjects. Negri (1991, 165) quotes Spinoza from the *Ethics*: "'Whatever so disposes the human Body that it can be affected in a great many ways, or renders it capable of affecting external Bodies in a great many ways, is useful to man; the more it renders the Body capable of being affected in a great many ways, or of affecting other bodies, the more useful it is; on the other hand, what renders the Body less capable of these things is harmful.' (Proposition 38)" (165).

One aspect of the multicultural classroom, in addition to the obvious one, that students from a variety of national, ethnic and class backgrounds are brought together, is the phenomenon of hybridity. An immigrant must be understood not only in relation to the country of origin, but also in terms of a hybrid identity which is generated by the juxtaposition of the original culture and the new culture. In her interview with Peter McLaren, Puiggros asks McLaren to discuss hybridization, both in the sense of multiple public spheres characterized by hybridity, and hybrid cultural identities:

> [T]eniendo en cuenta su interés por las hibridaciones y mixturas, por todo lo que está en los límites, por los problemas entre racionalidad e irracionalidad, entre mexicanos, americanos, chicanos y diferentes grupos, desde el punto de vista post y teniendo en cuenta ese interés suyo, piensa que en los EE.UU. y en México la mixtura y la hibridación tendrán un rol en el futuro de la educación? "Que ocurría cuando crezca este proceso de hibridación (McLaren 1992, 79)?

She asks, in short, if hybridity will have a role in the future of education. In the same interview, she asks whether or not there are social forces with the capacity to replace the state that could sustain the education of the majority of the population. These questions transcend the situation in Brazil and raise questions about the future of the state. In order to avoid an orthodox answer to the question about hybridity that would privilege social class over ethnicity, McLaren refers to the work of Ernesto Laclau and Homi Bhabha. He argues that

Chicanos, Latinos, African-Americans and Asians are articulating a cultural reality that contradicts capitalism. He writes that we live in a world of multiple "*alfabetismos,*" and that we are continually teaching ourselves these new languages. Thus, popular culture is a form of pedagogy (1992, 80). His distinction between a "metadiscourse" and a master discourse is very useful in the multicultural classroom. The former allows for a multiplicity of cultures while the latter forces a conformity grounded in colonialism.

I want to turn to McLaren and Rhonda Hammer's discussion of "media knowledges" for an example of an *alfabetismo.* According to McLaren and Hammer,

[a] critical media literacy recognizes that we inhabit a photocentric, aural, and televisual culture in which the proliferation of photographic and electronically produced images and sounds serve as a form of media catechism—perpetual pedagogy—through which individuals ritually encode and evaluate the engagements they make in the various discursive contexts of everyday life. This form of literacy understands media representations—whether photographs, television, print, film, or other forms—as productive not merely of knowledge but also of subjectivity (1992, 58).[2]

McLaren and Hammer explain the distorted view of reality presented by television:

George Gerbner (1989, 1990) has made a good case for the development of critical media literacy. His research has revealed that U.S. television accepts a distorted picture of the real world "more readily than itself." According to Gerbner, television reality is one in which men outnumber women three to one, where women are usually portrayed as either mothers or lovers, rarely work outside the home, and are natural victims of violence. It is a reality in which less than 10% of the population hold blue-collar jobs, where few elderly people exist, where Black youth learn to accept their minority status as inevitable and are trained to anticipate their own victimization (they are usually cast as the White hero's comic sidekick or a drug addicts, gang members, or killers). It is a world in which 18 acts of violence an hour occur in children's prime-time programs. Violence in television, Gerbner insists, demonstrates the social power of adult White males who are most likely to get involved with violence but most likely to get away with it. Television also serves as a mass spectacle reflecting and legitimating the allocative power of the state. That such an unreality could be rendered natural and commonsensical in a country that in 1990 reported the largest number of rapes against women in its history and a prison incarceration rate of Blacks that exceeds that of South Africa, where rich Angelenos are hiring private police, where wealthy neighborhoods display signs warning "Armed response!" and where security systems and the militarization of urban life are refiguring social space along the lines of the postmodern film *Bladerunner*, is symptomatic of a moral and epistemological crisis of astonishing proportions (McLaren and Hammer 1992, 46–47).

Because Gerbner is referring to the United States, and not Canada, one can only speculate about the sense of victimization on the part of the Anglophone Canadian in relation to the media, without referring to further research. Referring to their students and their comments after the Gulf War, McLaren and Hammer report:

> [O]ur students . . . expressed regret that they could no longer return to their television sets with the same mixture of commitment and enjoyment that many of them reserved only for their favorite soap operas. CNN's staged desire in its coverage of the war had presented them with unambiguous coordinates to construct national economies of affect in the form of binary oppositions (patriot/traitor; good/evil/ Christian/Muslim; democracy/dictatorship; liberators/enslaved) (1992, 54).

The border region provides the opportunity for border subjects to engage in critical media literacy by merely living a bicultural life. The news in Mexico is presented from a different viewpoint from the news in the United States. Although Mexico City tries to control media images throughout the country, as does Washington in the United States, there are gaps and slippages in border cities that occur as border crossers consume images and information from both cultures.

Examples of texts by Chicanos/as that teach literacies in McLaren's sense are Norma Iglesias's *Entre yerba, polvo y plomo, lo fronterizo visto por el cine mexicano*; Chon Noriega's *Chicanos and Film: Representation and Resistance* (1992); and Rosalinda Fregosos's *The Bronze Screen, Chicana and Chicano Film Culture* (1993). The first catalogues Mexican films regarding the border and exposes stereotypes; the second two delineate and analyze narrative codes and their complex interactions in Chicano film. Gutiérrez-Jones, in *Rethinking in the Borderlands* (1995), especially in its analysis of *American Me*, also teaches a gender literacy that calls on young Latinos to learn to mourn rather than to resort to violence. In order to do this they must develop rituals of mourning that are stronger than the desire to live up to the images of toughness which are romanticized in gang life.

McLaren and Hammer ask how "particular individuals throughout the course of their *every day* existence receive ritualized messages and integrate them on a daily basis (see McLaren 1985)" (1992, 59). Border dwellers received ritualized messages, in some cases, in two languages, from at least two and sometimes more cultural perspectives

(Anglo, Chicano/a, Mexican) and integrate them on a daily basis. At the time of this writing, the Chicano/a movement is gaining in strength and is engendering "a critical media literacy." Related to this movement are artists in the region whose art interrogates media images of Latinos. Thus, the region meets the criteria of being a community of resistance, a counter-public sphere, and a space in which "oppositional pedagogies that can resist dominant forms of meaning by offering new channels of communication, circuits of semiotic production, codifications of experience, and perspectives of reception that unmask the political linkage between images, their means of production and reception, and the social practices they legitimate" (McLaren and Hammer 1992, 59).

This multiplicity of cultures, communicated between students in a multicultural classroom, forms a magma from which emerges a multiplicity of subjectivities and a metadiscourse for talking about the formation and construction of one's own subjectivity. For example, Anzaldúa's *Borderlands* can help an Asian immigrant articulate his or her cultural reality *vis à vis* the dominant culture even though the Asian student may have little in common with Chicana lesbian culture. The film *The Joy Luck Club* can function similarly for an audience that includes Chicanas and Vietnamese of Chinese descent. In McLaren's *Life in Schools* (1989), he explains how he could have, in retrospect, given working class students assignments in which they interviewed people in their communities and analyzed the various problems in their lives. One advantage that the Chicano student in a Chicano Studies course has that Anglo students generally do not have is the possibility of a connection to a larger political movement. In San Diego, for example, elementary school children in bicultural schools are taught about human rights, farmworkers' struggles, and César Chávez. It is easier for the teacher to encourage them as university students to write about their own experiences within a political context because that context is visible outside of the classroom. Some of them have been exposed to the Chicano movement from elementary school all the way through Mecha in high school. On the other hand, in my experience teaching Anglo university students, it is difficult to get them to do what Aronowitz and Giroux feel is necessary, that is,

> providing students who have been constructed as "white" with the cultural memories that enable them to recognize that their own identities are the product of historical and social events and that class identities are obliterated by racial constructs. In part, this approach to multiculturalism as a cultural politics provides "white students" with self-definitions on which they can rec-

ognize whether they are speaking from within or outside privileged spaces. It also allows them to see how power works within and across differences to legitimate some voices and dismantle others (1994, 209).

Donaldo Macedo's *Literacies of Power* (1994) is a good example of the kind of information that should be provided to students who are not likely to have been exposed to it, but without a politicized movement in which Anglos are participating, on and off campus, it is difficult to convince the white students that they should even listen to what they may reject as the "radical ideas" of the professor learning many languages; rather, cultural literacies can be encouraged even without complete fluency another language. An example of a cultural literacy is the ability to read the languages that Robert Blauner (1996) refers to as the "two languages of race in America." In "The New Campus Racism," Noel Jacob Kent makes suggestions for a commitment to transformative education which seem to complement McLaren's teaching strategies. Quoting Blauner, Kent explains that the different languages of race must be part of the curriculum, along with other curriculum and policy changes such as the broadening of the canon, conflict mediation programs and opportunities for white students to experience "the daily realities of being 'otherness' by living in a majority African-American dorm" (1996, 55). The first language, according to Blauner, that of whites, "'locate[s] racism in color consciousness and its absence in color-blindness"; the second, that of Blacks, "expands the meaning to include power, position, and equality in the structuring of American society" (Kent 1996, 49, quoting Blauner 1996, n.p.). McLaren's notion of a "metadiscourse" provides the possibility for a context in which to discuss this difference in the two languages of race.

In his book *Literacies of Power*, Macedo describes the way in which the literacies taught in the school system in the United States stupefy the student population and keep it illiterate. He makes his own list of "what Americans need to know," a counterlist to E. D. Hirsch's. In the chapter entitled "English Only, The Tongue-Tying of America," he points out that if English were the guarantor of economic success that the English Only proponents claim it is, African-Americans would be enjoying economic success, since they are educated in English. Macedo addresses the "English Only" movement in the following passage:

> First, if English is the most effective educational language, how can we explain over 60 million Americans being illiterate or functionally illiterate? Sec-

ond, if education in "English only" can guarantee linguistic minorities a better
future, as educators like William Bennett promise, why do the majority of
Black Americans, whose ancestors have been speaking English for over two
hundred years, find themselves still relegated to ghettos? (1994, 127)

He then argues that linguistic, racial, and sex discrimination, and the
way in which subjects are located within different social cultural and
economic positions, are much more useful in developing effective teaching methods than the reduction of the problem to the issue of the
English language (Macedo 1994, 127).

One way of looking at multiple literacies is to consider the perspectives available in the multicultural classroom as they are discussed by
Kincheloe in *Toward a Critical Politics of Teacher Thinking (1993)*.
Kincheloe uses the metaphor of holography (160) to discuss multiple
perspectives, as I do in *Border Writing* (Hicks, 1991, xxix, 1988,
54–56, 1985, 20). Kincheloe writes:

[P]ost-formal teachers begin to look at the lessons from the perspectives of
their black students, their Hispanic students, their white students, their poor
students, their middle-class and upper-middle class students, their tradition-
ally successful students, their unsuccessful students (1993, 161).

Kincheloe also refers to liberation theologians, who, he writes, assert
that the "way to find an alternative to the mainstream perspective . . .
is to understand an institution from the vantage point of those who
have suffered most as the result of its existence" (1993, 161).

McLaren's notion of "metadiscourse" could allow for a discussion
in the classroom of a chapter title of Macedo's, "Our Uncommon Culture: The Politics of Race, Class, Gender and Language." Although
Macedo spends most of this chapter questioning Freire about issues
of gender and race, the title brings together the concerns we have
considered to this point. There are different languages of race which
undermine the idea of a common culture; similarly, there are different
languages of class and gender. As revealed by the dialogue "Ghetto
Life 101," which was broadcast on National Public Radio and is discussed by Macedo, the lived experiences of teachers and students usually differ drastically.

McLaren's discussion of "metadiscourse" is interesting when read
in relation to the work of Spinoza in his *Ethics*, particularly his discussion of reason and his theory of affects and its link to power. Spinoza's
reason is not a master discourse; rather, it allows for a multiplicity of
discourses. The "metadiscourse" in a classroom can allow for a multi-

plicity of viewpoints. Multiple literacies can help us to transmute the "sad" encounter into the "joyful" encounter; multiple literacies can help us to develop an adequate rather than a confused idea. Because the media can transform us at the affective level, it can also help us to change the "sad" encounter described by Spinoza into a "joyful" encounter by helping us to get an adequate idea rather than a confused idea; conversely, the media can keep us in a confused state. This transformation can bring one from a state of passivity to the ability to act, or the reverse. The transformation of paralyzing negative emotions into joyful affects that allow us to act is described by Anzaldúa in relation to the experience of the Coatlicue state.

Many other educators besides McLaren have argued that the multicultural classroom demands new curriculum and new teaching methods, that is, a multicultural approach to teaching; one area of research in which multiculturalism has been debated is literary theory. While Aronowitz and Giroux, in *Education Still under Siege*, attempt to "recontextualize the debate . . . in order to reappropriate its democratic and utopian possibilities as part of a progressive educational agenda" (1994, 195), M. Keith Booker, in *A Practical Introduction to Literary Theory and Criticism*, gives an overview of multicultural literary criticism. Booker begins by pointing out that "writers working outside the long dominant white European cultural tradition have become a major force—or many, the major force—in contemporary world literature" (1996, 150). He continues: "Multicultural theorists have demonstrated the historical complicity of the canon and of literary studies in racism, imperialism, and the general cultural domination by Western Europe and North America of most of the rest of the world" (151). Booker situates two critics on opposite ends of the spectrum regarding the question of which language a writer should use. On one end is Salman Rushdie, who argues that writers from "former British colonies should seek to adapt English to their particular situations and thereby 'decolonize' the language" (quoted in Booker, 152). This position has something in common with that of Deleuze and Guattari in *Kafka*, in which they call for a different use of the dominant language, a "minor" use. On the other end is Ngugi wa Thiong'o, who believes that, according to Booker, "Africans will never be able to establish a strong sense of self as long as they continue to express their deepest thoughts in European languages" (152). In border culture, these debates occur in the Chicano/a community: some Chicanos/as write only in English, some in both English and Spanish, and some write only in Spanish.

For the Kenyan writer Ngugi, language cannot be separated from a sense of self. Booker refers to Fredric Jameson's essay "Third World Literature in the Era of Multinational Capitalism" (1986), in which Jameson argues that the major characters in "'third world texts' . . . must necessarily be read as 'national allegories'" (quoted in Booker 1996, 155). Booker explains Jameson's rationale:

> [There is a] lack of the clear separation between public and private realms typical of Western societies [which] effaces the boundary between individual characters and the societies in which they live, leading to a situation in which 'the story of a private individual destiny is always an allegory of the embattled situation of the public third-world culture and society' (Booker 1996, 155).

According to Booker, Bhabha goes further, and calls for "an 'unseating [of] the Transcendental subject'" (155). From a border perspective, Deleuze and Guattari's definition of the deterritorialized subject as existing in a reality in which everything is political, is more useful than Jameson's linking of the character to a national allegory. In terms of pedagogical theory, these debates take the form of the relation of language, culture, and self- esteem in the classroom. Many argue that self-esteem is crucial, and that bilingual education, and now Ebonics, is an important part of the building of self-esteem. Henry Louis Gates, Jr., in an address to the American Council of Learned Societies K–12 Literacy Project (1994), took an opposing point of view with regard to the teaching of self-esteem in the classroom; he argued that content, not self-esteem, was what African-American children needed to learn.

In "The Intellectual as a Contemporary Phenomenon" (1992, 1997), Paul Bové juxtaposes Ngugi and Jameson. He recalls a conference at University of California, San Diego in the summer of 1991 in which Jameson made the argument, as Bové understood it, "that given the global nature of the market in Late Capitalism, even so-called 'third-world intellectuals' aspire to a place in the global market, as evidenced by example, their speaking in English and wanting to be translated into English" (1992, 1997, 8). Bové puts forward the counterexample of Ngugi as a supporter of "efforts to produce local cultures, often regional in nature, based on communities that cross nation-state borders or operate in open defiance of state power" (8). From the perspective of the U.S.-Mexico border, Chicano/a culture and border culture could be seen in similar terms.

One charge leveled against postmodernism is that it relativizes all in its purview. As McLaren writes in regard to subaltern and feminist challenges to the postmodern critique: "[Paul] Gilroy [1990, 278] points out that widely publicized views of the postmodern condition held by such prominent critics as Fredric Jameson may simply constitute another form of Eurocentric master narrative since black expressive cultures use all the new technological means at their disposal 'not to flee from depth but to revel in it, not to abjure public history but to proclaim it'" (Gilroy quoted in McLaren 1993, 197). Quite significantly for our discussion, McLaren also links nationalism to debates about the "subject" (197). Booker outlines some of these debates as well. In their essay "Feminism and Postmodernism," Nancy Fraser and Linda Nicholson point out that feminists have continued to focus on political practice, while the "postmodern conception of criticism without philosophy" of J. Lyotard, the postmodernist on whom they choose to focus, "rule[s] out several recognizable genres of social criticism" (1988, 379).

If affirmative action is able to bring together students from different cultural backgrounds, and if this can contribute to the learning of the kinds of multiple literacies, then why is it being dismantled? One blatant attack, in addition to legislation, is Herrnstein and Murray's book *The Bell Curve* (1994). In response to this book, Catherine A. Lugg, in her essay "Attacking Affirmative Action: Social Darwinism as Public PRolicy," [PR refers to public relations] explains how politically conservative white Americans have historically defined themselves as "the advanced race" (1996, 369). She writes:

> Thanks to the influence of social Darwinism upon American social thought, the real game of 'survival of he fittest' was fixed. During a time when many decent work opportunities were limited to white Protestants, the meritocratic mythology was as powerful as it was pernicious. This notion of economic success, if not outright salvation, through hard work also drove much of the belief systems of white Protestants (1996, 371).

She also points out that white women have been the biggest beneficiaries of affirmative action, and yet they are left out of Herrnstein and Murray's book.

Despite the dismantling of affirmative action, the number of Latino students in the entering class at the state university in the U.S.-Mexico border region, San Diego State University, continues to grow. There is a high drop-out rate of Latino university students, however, just as there is of Latino high school students, or as McLaren notes, what "Latino students rightly call . . . 'push-out' rate[s] (1994, 143). While some Anglo parents complain about affirmative action, many Latino parents complain that they too are taxpayers, and yet their children receive inferior educations.

How do the educational system and the curriculum continue to reinforce colonial relations? For example, how does the "English Only" movement function in relation to the lives of Latino students? McLaren writes:

> Donaldo Macedo rightly claims [it] is undergirding dominant forms of school-ing that function and legitimate Anglocentric values and meaning and at the same time negate the history, culture, and language practices of minority students. It has its roots in Europe's demonization of dark-skinned populations—one that pits the Anglo "I" against the dark, forbidding "Other" (1994, 141).

A critical approach to canonical works of literature can undermine the reinforcement of colonial relations. For example, the demonization of dark-skinned populations in nineteenth century England of the Irish and the Welsh is described by Charlotte Bronte, in *Jane Eyre*. Bronte points to the simian nature of Rochester, as critic Elsie Michie points out in her essay, "White Chimpanzees and Oriental Despots: Racial Stereotyping and Edward Rochester." (1996). McLaren explains Foucault's view that power both subjectivizes and subjugates. In Chapter Three, "The Teaching of Bilingual Students," I will discuss linguistic purity, whiteness, and how power can function in both of these ways. McLaren also raises the question to be raised by the critical researcher: "Whose interests are being served in the social act of becoming liter-ate?" Conversely, I will ask whose interests are being served to pre-vent bilingual education?

In his essay "In the Name of Science and of Genetics and of The Bell Curve: White Supremacy in American Schools," Ladislaus Semali argues that

> current efforts in American schools to introduce multicultural curricula should, therefore, be encouraged. A critical multiculturalism should be more reflexive with respect to the different social groups in the United States and the rela-tionships of developments in the United States to the rest of the world. This would mean, for instance, that we begin to see the issue of racial inequality in global and relational terms in the context of what Immanuel Wallerstein calls "world systems theory" (Wallerstein, 1990). The links between America's de-velopment and the underdevelopment of poor countries of the world and the links that African-Americans had had in terms of their intellectual and politi-cal engagement with the people of Africa must be emphasized. This will not be achieved by emphasizing exoticism and cultural differences associated with so-called primitive humanity (1995, 174).

A challenge for the critical teacher is to avoid "a celebration of differ-ence without investigating the ways in which difference or diversity becomes constituted in oppressive asymmetrical relations of power

. . . [that] often betray a simple-minded romanticism and exoticization of the 'Other'" (McLaren 994, 146).

Aronowitz's discussion of Freire is useful at this point in our discussion of social justice and relations of power. He writes:

> Freire warns against defining the goal of radical movements exclusively in terms of social justice and a more equitable society, since these objectives can be partially achieved without shared decision-making, especially over knowledge and political futures. The key move away from the old elitist conception in which the intellectuals play a dominant role is to challenge the identity of power with the state (1994, 234).

I began this chapter with a discussion of a model of the good classroom and then raised the question of what the effect of the hybrid would have on education. I introduced McLaren's notion of "multiple literacies" as a goal of education. I have argued that Spinoza's "good" City can be expanded to the good classroom, and I have referred to critical pedagogy, multiculturalism, and postmodernism. If postmodernism is understood as merely another colonial discourse, as has been argued by some critics, then it is understandable that those who have suffered from colonialism would be wary of it. I have attempted to pose the question differently and to reveal an alternative tradition of democracy that is not dependent on modernism, specifically, Spinoza's notion of the "good" City. In this framing of the issues, it has been in the era of modernism that alternative discourses have been silenced. As some countries enter the postmodern era, there are new opportunities for postmodern pedagogy. The border dweller has a unique opportunity in the postmodern era to participate in postmodern, pedagogical experiments. McLaren and Hammer define a critical media literacy, in part, as how individuals receive "ritualized" messages in their daily lives. I have argued that in addition to the strategies suggested by McLaren and Hammer, along with others, for acquiring critical media literacy, border dwellers have an opportunity to maintain a skeptical, critical stance towards the dominant culture because they are situated between two cultures. A border region by definition delegitimates the power of the state, creating fissures between knowledge, power and the state. The border scholar and teacher can learn from the border student, who has often been exposed to more varied cultural codes in the multicultural classroom than has the teacher.

In parts of the United States such as California, demographic shifts have created new linguistic, ethnic, religious, cultural, and class boundaries. This mixture and hybridization can have a profound and beneficial effect on the education of students of all cultures. This multiplicity of cultures, communicated between students, forms a magma from which emerges a multiplicity of subjectivities and a metadiscourse for talking about the formation and construction of one's own subjectivity. Just as feminism not only helps women, but men as well, to articulate the ways in which they perform their gender roles, and are sometimes oppressed by these roles, so critical literacies help Anglo students, not just Latino and other non-Anglo students, to recognize the ways in which they perform social roles within a racialized class system.

In my view, attacks on affirmative action and attempts to dismantle it signal: (1) a fear of the Other; (2) an attempt to reinforce colonial relations; (3) evidence that the state is no longer able to educate the majority of its population; and (4) an ambivalence about creating a truly democratic society. Nevertheless, I agree with Freire that the call for "social justice and a more equitable society," with which affirmative action shares an affinity, is necessary but not sufficient for the profound radical social changes suggested by Freire's pedagogy. The reason is that, as Freire points out, social justice and an equitable society may be "partially achieved" without "shared decision-making." Therefore, not only must the punitive, racist political legislation such as Proposition 187 and 209 and the English the Official Language movement be fought, and affirmative action be defended, but "shared decision-making" as well must be foregrounded as a goal. "Shared decision-making" is more likely to take place in an environment in which subjects with a multiplicity of perspectives are able to engage in pleasant encounters; the good classroom, based on Spinoza's "good" City, can be one of these environments.

Notes

1. See Michael Hardt's discussion of these terms in his "Translator's Foreword," *The Savage Anomaly* (1991).

2. See Giroux and McLaren (1991), 18–33; McLaren (1988), 213–34; and McLaren (1986).

Chapter 3

Literacy and the Teaching of Literature for Bilingual and Bicultural Students

I want to consider the challenges faced by the teacher of literature for bilingual students and for these students at both the K–12 and university levels. My argument will be that the white subject, the only subject valorized in the field of English in the United States, needs to take its place as one of many in the classroom rather than as a cultural dominant, and that this can take place through the: (1) teaching of multicultural literature as a form of teaching literacy; (2) the training of teachers to become multicultural; (3) the use of ritual in which both the teach and the student can develop a context for reflexivity about the self and ethnicity and the student can understand how he or she has been coded as a subject in the culture; and (4) the utilization of the knowledge within bicultural communities in the classroom. I will look at the use of literature in the multicultural classroom in relation to cultural identity and sensitivity of students of all backgrounds. Although I will focus on the effect on bilingual and bicultural students, I will consider the effect on all students, at the university level, of the division between rhetoric and literature departments. I will attend to degrees of bilingualism, and attitudes in immigrant communities, including the Latino/a community, regarding language. Teachers in the multicultural classroom need to be educated about language acquisition as well as the demographic shifts in the United States and their effects on the classroom of the next century. The U.S.-Mexico border provides an opportunity to speculate about optimum conditions for the teaching of literature for bilingual and bicultural students, regardless of the degree of bilingualism or biculturalism. This will include a discussion of learning styles and values. Ruth Buchanan, in "Border Crossings, NAFTA, Regulatory Restructuring and the Politics of Place,"

(1995), argues that border regions are characterized by contradictory tendencies, and I will explore these by considering conflicting attitudes of educators, administrators, counselors, parents and community activists. Some of these conflicting attitudes in the U.S.-Mexico border region include attacks on bilingual education, an emphasis on drop-out rates, and a concern with the legal status of immigrant children.[1] The backdrop for this discussion will be globalism in the era of late capitalism, and capital's need to forge subjectivities as commodities.

The definition of literacy I will use comes from Donaldo Macedo in *Literacies of Power*. He rejects "instrumental literacy" in favor of the ability to "read the world":

> The instrumental literacy for the poor, in the form of a competency-based skills-banking approach, and the highest form of instrumental literacy for the rich, acquired through the university in the form of professionalization, share one common feature: They both prevent the development of the critical thinking that enables one to "read the world" critically and to understand the reasons and linkages behind the facts (1994, 16).

In her essay "Chicano Bilingualism," Rosaura Sánchez delineates four types of bilingualism, taken from Glyn Lewis (1972). The most relevant to the U.S.-Mexico border is stable bilingualism. The last three categories are dynamic, transitional and vestigial. An example of stable bilingualism is found in everyday life in the border region. Many Chicanos/as who speak little or no Spanish still call their children "*m'jo*" or "*m'ja*," which are shortened forms of "*mi hijo*" or "*mi hija*." Students with the opportunity to travel or who have been forced to relocate make up the other three categories, as do some Chicanos. The most economically privileged of these would be students who travel with the intent of learning other languages and who would choose to take a bilingual or bicultural class based on their profound familiarity with another culture. Transitional bilingualism, in which "two or more languages assume overlapping function," which in turn "inevitably leads to the exclusive use of one language for those functions," continues to be a part of the debates surrounding bilingual education. Many bilingual teachers justify the use of Spanish as a transition to English. Vestigial bilingualism, according to Sánchez, applies to a "large number of fourth, fifth and sixth generation Chicanos who have assimilated completely to the English language but still retain a few words or expressions as ethnic markers" (Sánchez 1977, 210).

Another perspective on bilingualism can be found in research on "code switching." What is interesting about the use of two linguistic codes, in this case Spanish and English, is that it appears to follow certain rules. The decision to use certain phrases because they are more effective in capturing or expressing what the speaker wants to express can be found in bilingual novels such as Jessica Hagedorn's novel *Dogeaters* (1990) and in Italian-American novels. It is not necessary to emphasize a distinction between biculturalism and bilingualism. Rather, what is important is how these processes exist and interact in the classroom.

The context for all of these kinds of bilingualism is a double standard of bilingualism that Susan J. Dicker describes in her essay "Ten Official Arguments and Counter-Arguments" (1977). She points out that there are two kinds of blingualism, "elite" and "folk"; what distinguishes them is social class. She quotes Rosalie Pedalino Porter:

> For the immigrant recently arrived, bilingualism is an uncomfortable, imperfect phase on the way to somewhere else. Knowing and using a different language at home have historically been seen as signs of being 'lower class.' Bilingualism that is valued is the elite variety—full competency in two languages among a small percentage of people for the purpose of scholarly work, diplomacy, foreign trade, or travel. (Dicker 1997, quoting Porter 1997, n.p.).

As Dicker points out, there is no logical reason why both kinds of bilingualism cannot be seen as useful and positive, If, in the case of elite bilingualism, there is nothing transitional about the ability to be fully fluent in two languages, and this is considered to be a lifelong advantage, then why should "folk" bilingualism be seen as transitional? Dicker also notes that the distinction between "foreign" and "immigrant" or "minority" languages reveals the same double standard. In the U.S.-Mexico border region, it is clear that the distinction is one of class, but that in addition, racism plays a factor. As Steven Krashen's (1982) work suggests, if Mexico were France, Anglo San Diegans would learn French with enthusiasm and dedication.

The theoretical approach employed in this chapter will draw on the work of Gloria Anzaldúa, Deleuze and Guattari, Vine Deloria, Stephen Krashen, Paulo Freire, Kris Gutiérrez, Lisa Delpit, Donaldo Macedo, Peter McLaren, Luis Moll, and Negri. The literary examples will come from works by Gloria Anzaldúa, Alma E. Cervantes, Sandra Cisneros, Diana Engel, Louise Erdich, David Hwang, Carmen Lomas Garza, Aylette Jenness, Naguib Mahfouz, Carlos Pellicer López, Cherríe Moraga, Naomi Quiñónes, and Helena Viramontes. I hope to undermine the tendency in current debates in pedagogy to separate theoretical discussion from what might be useful to a teacher in a classroom. The discussion of literature provides an excellent opportunity to do this, because the decisions about how literature should be taught and which literature should be taught raise theoretical questions in pedagogy which go beyond the field of English. More importantly, teaching literature can become a valuable tool for teaching literacy in the larger sense of the term of reading the world and understand one's position in it.

The teaching of multicultural literature can be a form of teaching literacy. In Anzaldúa's children's book *Friends from the The Other Side, Amigos del otro lado* (1993), the main character, who is a young Chicana, befriends a boy who is a recent immigrant from Mexico. The book can be used to generate discussions about which point of view is more dominant, the Chicana's or the Mexican's, and how this functions in counterpoint to the multicultural message. The backgrounds of readers in a classroom will raise the infinitely complex relationship between and attitudes about Anglos and Latinos/as, and Chicanos/as and recent immigrants.

Reading the gendered Latino world and understanding her position in it is central in the work of Alma Cervantes. In the poem "Had I Ironed Your Shirt?," Cervantes writes "Had I ironed your shirt, maybe you'd still be here by my side" (1996, 132). Although out of context, this could be read as sarcastic, bitter, and without regret, but within the poem, the phrase is much more poignant. As in Cervantes's "Piquetitos of Love," we find ambivalence rather than a logical feminist stance: "*Lo hizo porque me ama*/He did it because he loves me . . ." (1996, 128). Although she has been beaten by her lover, she stays, and prays that one day he "will fall out of love for me." Until then, she awaits "the blood that streams from the wounds of [his] loving" (1996, 129).

Cultural diversity is addressed by Sandra Cisneros in a short story and by Aylette Jenness in a children's book, *Ven a mi casa: una búsqueda de tesoro multicultural* (1993). The complexity of the *mestizaje* can be seen in Cisneros's *House on Mango Street* (1994) in the story "Hair." The mixture of the indigenous, the European and the African in the Latino population are signified by qualities of different types of hair. Cultural diversity spanning many neighborhoods can be found in Jenness's *Ven a mi casa, una búsqueda de tesoro multicultural*. Two projects grew out of a video that author Jenness and Joanne Rizzi made with a group of children and adults in Boston: the book, and a traveling exhibition entitled "Kids Bridge." There is also a series of books entitled Kids Bridge, of which *Ven a mi casa* is a part. Four children, or guides, Abdus, Annie, Marco and Terri, lead the reader through different neighborhoods in Boston. The authors, Jenness and Rizzi, explain that the reader will probably find similar areas in the city in which she or he resides. The neighborhoods explored are African American, Irish-American, Latino (Puerto Rican) and Cambodian. Marco introduces the reader to important foods in Latino neighborhoods, such as bananas, and specific ways of cooking them, such as fried bananas. Abdus leads the reader to a store, Nubian Notion, with African medallions and baskets, to the Museum of the National Center for African-American Artists, and to the African Tropical Forest in the Boston Zoo. Terry looks for a Cambodian fruit, *rambutan*, in her neighborhood; there are kosher stores as well as Cambodian markets in her neighborhood. Annie is from an Irish-American neighborhood. She goes to buy bread and to look for a *claddagh* (a heartshaped ring); she also takes the reader to the Catholic Church San Ambrosio. The book explains that during the Irish potato famine, husbands and wives exchanged rings when the husband went to America in search of a better life. The heart signifies love, the hands friendship, and the crown loyalty. The book also explains how to make a video: (1) investigating an area in order to identify special areas of interest; (2) getting releases to videotape people; (3) limiting the places and people to a smaller number, such as five; (4) keeping in mind how you want the tape to start, perhaps on a main street or a well-known place; (5) deciding whether or not to have a voice-over narrator; (6) deciding on an ending; (7) keeping the tape to fifteen minutes. Finally, the book has a glossary, with words such as Buddhist, generation, ethnic group, immigrant, kosher and prejudice. The narrative structure of the book is interactive. The reader can get more in-depth information by turning to appropriate papers, or he or she can read a simplified version of the story. The book was published in conjunction with an exhibition at the Children's Museum in Boston. In the U.S.-Mexico border region, a similar book could be produced by students in which Latino, African-American, Vietnamese, Italian and Mexican neighborhoods on both sides of the border could be documented. Students could also make videotapes. An exhibition could be held at a school or a cultural center, such as the Centro Cultural de la Raza.

For the Spanish-speaking child, a book which encourages reflexivity about one's world is Carlos Pellicer López's *Julieta y su caja de colores* (1984), published in Mexico. In *Ven a mi casa*, the four narrators guide the reader through their neighborhoods. In *Julieta y su caja de colores*, Julieta paints her city. She feels that with her water colors she can see on paper that which she cannot see with her eyes. A bicultural reality as represented in multicultural literature often includes a focus on common themes such as food and art, as is illustrated in Carmen Lomas Garza's *Family Pictures, Cuadros de familia* (1980). "Picking Nopal Cactus" depicts a family, grandparents, a mother and a son, picking cactus. The story describes how the grandfather removed the spines and the grandmother cooked the cactus by parboiling it in water and then cooking it with eggs and chili powder for breakfast the next morning. In "Making Tamales," the entire family is shown engaged in all phases of the process, from soaking the dried leaves from the corn to cooling the rolled and folded tamales. Lomas Garza explains that in some families, only the women make tamales, but in hers, everyone helps. In the final story, "Beds for Dreaming," Lomas Garza describes the way in which she and her sister used to go on the roof on summer nights and talk about their futures. Lomas Garza knew by the time that she was thirteen years old that she wanted to be an artist, and she credits her mother for being the one who inspired her: " She made up our beds to sleep in and have regular dreams, but she also laid out the bed for our dreams of the future." (1990, 30). Art and dreams are also linked in *Julieta y su caja de colores*. Pellicer López writes: "*Como los magos que hacen aparecer conejos en los sombreros . . . así ella, con sus colores, hacía aparecer ciudades . . . y suenos en su cuaderno*" (1984, 14). In Engel's *Gino Badino* (1991), an Italian American child struggles against the boring constraints of a family business; eventually, his artistic nature is accepted by the family as his creativity is incorporated into the family pasta business. His pasta sculptures are included in the packages of pasta.

In the stories just considered, both boys and girls are articulate and intelligent; both are able to express themselves as artists. Men and women are shown working together in the kitchen making tamales in Lomas Garza's *Family Pictures*, revealing that there are gender relations in traditional Latino culture that might be considered "best practices" when contrasted with Anglo culture. These works reflect a tendency towards more progressive, enlightened views about gender in texts being written for younger children. In literature written for adults, such as Cisneros's *House on Mango Street*, and works included in the anthology *Chicana Creativity and Criticism*, more painful issues about gender and social class in the Latina community are raised, although often with a sense of humor. Naomi Quiñónes in *"Ay que María Felix* (or María was No Virgin)" (1996) refers to a binary opposition, without mentioning it directly, that is known to her bicultural readers: the opposition between the Mexican Golden Age of Cinema stars María Felix and Dolores del Río. The image in the Mexican imagination of Felix is that of the *mujer sufrida*, who suffers whatever befalls her with grace, elegance, and dignity. Her sexuality is rarefied and understated in the beauty of the "arched eyebrow/arrogant tilt of head." Dolores del Río, on the other hand, is seen as the temperamental, fiery, overtly sexual woman. Quiñónes deconstructs the virgin/whore dichotomy, or mother/lover dichotomy, suggested by these two, in her subtitle "María was No Virgin" and in the description of the "black/soft wool clinging/lace collar high/and plunging backline/lower than the San Joaquin Valley (1996, 102)." She does not reveal cleavage, as Dolores del Rio would, but neither is she completely covered in a shawl.

While María Felix played characters of different social classes, Helena Viramontes (1996, 164–68), evokes working-class culture. The story begins with a mother and daughter shopping for cosmetics at K-Mart. "Miss Clairol" has a special significance for me because, first, it is set in the fifties, when I grew up; second, my mother dyed her hair blonde; and third, my mother, who has been married four times, dated a lot during my childhood. What hurt me in my childhood was that my mother, whose natural hair color was brown, did not want to look like me; brown hair was not good enough. However, Viramontes's daughter, Champ, is not concerned with such thoughts. Rather, she and her mother, Arlene, are co-conspirators, both dedicated to the task of making Arlene beautiful for her night out. Nevertheless, an aura of emotional discomfort surrounds sexuality in the descriptions of the first sexual experiences of the mother and the daughter. In the case of the mother, she is disgusted by Puppet, who ejaculates prematurely all over her legs and belly.

In "Red Clowns," Cisneros describes the narrator's first sexual experience, rape. There is a sense of betrayal, disillusionment and abandonment. The character feels that the older generation of women should have prepared her to defend herself. I have argued that teaching literature can become a valuable tool for teaching literacy in the larger sense of the term of reading the world and understand one's position in it. In a very poignant way, this is clear in a passage by Cherríe Moraga from her play "Giving up the Ghost":

> Got raped once. When I was a kid. Taken me a long time to say that was
> exactly what happened . . . Makes you more aware than ever that you are
> one hunerd percent female, just in case you had any doubts one hunerd per-
> cent female whether you act it or like it or not. (1983)

The humiliation of social class is included in Cisneros's *House on Mango Street* when a nun asks the narrator, "You live there?" In another story, the narrator listens to a friend complain about "those" people moving into the neighborhood, knowing that she, the narrator, is one of those people.

Not only can the teaching of multicultural literature be a form of teaching literacy, but it can be part of the teacher's education in becoming multicultural. At UCLA, teachers were exposed to Hwang's *M. Butterfly* (1986), Mahfouz' *Palace Walk* (1990), and Erdrich's *Tracks* (1988). Part of the teaching of teachers to become multicultural has to do with the transformation of the classroom from an at-risk environment to an optimal environment. Nadeen T. Ruiz, Erminda García and Richard A. Figueroa, in *The Ole Curriculum Guide* (n.d.), list two types of environments. In the at-risk environment, the directions are given by the teacher to the student, and there is an expectation of "correct" behavior from the beginning. In terms of assessment, there is a letter grade and the emphasis on a single, correct answer. The classroom focuses on the individualism and the teacher has limited expectations of students. In the optimal environment for culturally and linguistically diverse students in both general and special education, there is a very different kind of classroom. Topics are suggested by students and materials are student centered. There is a whole-part-whole approach to the text rather than a fragmented approach. Active student participation is encouraged. There is a focus on ideas before mechanics. Work is done for a purpose (authentic purpose), not for the teacher. The student is immersed in language and print. Both teachers and students (peers) present and demonstrate information rather than directions being given by the teacher alone. In terms of assessment, immediate response is given rather than a letter grade or an emphasis on a single, correct answer. The classroom is seen as a learning community and teachers have high expectations for all students. (Ruiz, Garcia, and Figueroa, 5)

As Deborah Dietrich and Kathleen S. Ralph argue "[C]ultural definitions of the American self have long been presumed to be White" (Morrison, 1992, quoted in Dietrich and Ralph 1995). They conclude that classrooms need to be "lively forums" of a variety of cultural viewpoints, and that this needs to be supported through the selection of materials that allow students to become "multiculturally sensitive" (6). Literature can play a role in creating the multicultural classroom in that faculty can, and they argue must, "empower literary works outside the traditional texts in order to prepare students to live in their increasingly culturally diverse society" (1995, 6).

Nevertheless, Kris Gutiérrez, in her interview/dialogue with Peter McLaren, argues that literacy instruction continues to function as a way of socializing historically marginalized students into particular forms of knowing and being that make access to critical forms and practices of literacy in either their first or second language difficult." (1995, 131). An example of how the contemporary classroom silences critical multicultural voices can be found in a story Gutiérrez relates in the same interview about her twelve-year-old biracial son. In a discussion of Mecca in her son's geography class, the teacher showed a clip of Malcolm X from the film *X*; the teacher asked the students to point out what was most important in the clip. Gutiérrez's son said, "'Well, I think that the fact that Malcolm is being followed by two white CIA agents as he goes to worship is very interesting.'" Gutierrez explains that he was "publicly chastised for being off-topic" (1995, 127).

How are we to understand the rationale for (1) denying access to a literacy that could allow students to understand how they coded into the culture and (2) capitalism's "selection" of a self in Brian Massumi's sense: "A self is selected (produced and consumed) (1993, 22)"? In other words, why would a capitalist system allow an educational system to be so ineffective, and why would the production of a reflexive self be discouraged by this system? McLaren writes that

> [c]apitalism has colonized all geographial and social space and schools have not been immune . . . . Massumi argues that capitalism is coextensive with its own inside, such that it has now become field of both immanence and exteriority. There is no escape. There is only fear. Fear, reports Massumi, is now the objective condition of subjectivity in the era of late capitalism. In this sense it means something more than a fear of downward mobility but rather the constitution of the self within a market culture and market morality. When nonmarket values—such as love and compassion—disappear from everyday life nihilism sets in. Cornel West speaks eloquently about this dilemma, especially in urban settings (1995, 130).

Massumi explains:

> Bodies are selected, on the basis of certain socially valorized distinctions, for priority access to a certain kind of apparatus. African-American men, for

example, are favored for prison and the army on the basis of their skin color. Women of all races are favored for biopower on the basis of gender: the medicalization of childbirth and social engineering of the child-rearing responsibilities women still disproportionately bear. Priority access to one apparatus of actualization does not necessarily exclude a body's selection by another. The same body can, inevitably is, selected for different apparatuses successively and simultaneously. Prison follows school follows family (1993, 21).

The link between capitalist values and the expectations teachers have about non-Anglo students is documented and discussed in the work of Swisher (1994). She found that "non Indians were more likely to consider indifference to work ethic and indifference to ownership as values which have a significant effect on either an American Indian student's approach or demonstration of learning because of the perceived compatibility with the mainstream American work ethic and attitude toward individual ownership" (9).[2] Research results in the study that are relevant to the Chicano community in the San Diego-Tijuana border region have to do with the finding that "American Indian respondents selected discipline, group harmony, holistic approach to health, and spirituality to a greater extent than non-Indians."

As a teacher, I have found that many Chicano/a students are committed to these values as well, especially in the Chicana community. Altar-building for the Day of the Dead celebrations and as part of art installations is part of the context for this finding outside of the classroom. In two Mexican-American studies classes I have taught recently, these values have been brought into the classroom as well by students. In one case, Ramón Flores, a Native American activist with a highly developed sense of ethics and values who is also gay and an ex-priest, explained to the class during a presentation that he was part of an organization dedicated to bringing accurate information about Native American and Native American values into the classroom. He built an altar in the class, explained the role of healing in Native American communities, and, at the request of an Anglo student, did a *limpia* [healing ritual] with her after the class. In another class, a Chicana activist with a background in *teatro* brought up the values of non-competition (group harmony) in relation to a discussion of Chicano artists who had become obsessed with careers. She also explained the importance of the extended family, a holistic approach to health, a respect for nature, spirituality, patience, placidity, and cooperation in the context of a class discussion of *Borderlands* and Hernandez's graphic novel *Blood of Palomar*. Both books evoke rage in the Chicano community. In *Blood of Palomar*, rage takes various forms in the highly complex cast of characters. In *Borderlands*, rage and pain are part of both the form and the content of Anzaldúa's autobiographical sections. Nevertheless, *Borderlands* does emphasize the importance of spirituality.

Parla argues that changing demographics suggest that all teachers will be faced with a multicultural student body, and one that is no longer dominated by European immigrants, but, in the last ten years, by students from Asia, Central America and the Caribbean. She calls on teachers to prepare themselves by adopting a three-part model which consists of (1) the Theoretical Base; (2) the Linguistic and Cultural Diversity Base and (3) the Experiential base. For our purposes, it is the theoretical base that is of greatest interest. Parla refers to a compilation of definitions in Banks and McGee-Banks (1993) and Bennett (1990) of the term "multicultural education"; it enhances higher-order thinking and problem-solving skills; increases academic performance of all students; increases awareness and knowledge of the history, culture, and perspectives of all ethnic and racial groups, enhances students' self-esteem, self-awareness, and identity; promotes the valuing of cultural differences so that they are viewed in an egalitarian mode rather than in an inferior/superior mode; and develops an understanding of the multicultural nation and interdependent world (Parla 1994, 2).

Parla also refers to Banks's proposed six stages of ethnicity. It is only in the latter three that the abilities to live in a multicultural, multiethnic world emerge. In the earlier stages, the painful journey from self-loathing leads to separatism. The first, Ethnic Psychological Captivity, is characterized by the internalization of negative societal beliefs about one's own ethnic groups. The second, Ethnic Encapsulation, consists of an ethnocentric attitude and the practice of ethnic separatism. The third, Ethnic Identity Clarification, marks a shift towards an openness to other ethnicities: one accepts one's own ethnicity and clarifies one's attitudes toward one's own ethnic group. The fourth, Biethnicity, describes the ability, in terms of attitudes, skill and commitment, to participate both within one's own ethnic group and another ethnic group or culture. The fifth, Multiethnicity and Reflective Nationalism, is an extension of the fourth; a reflexive attitude about one's own ethnic and cultural background allows one to co-exist with within a range of ethnic and cultural groups in one's own nation.

Finally, the sixth, Globalism and Global Competency, is the culmination of the other five: one has the ability to function within cultures not only in one's own nation but also in the world. (Parla 1994, 3, referring to Banks 1994).

Considered in relation to the U.S.-Mexico border and Chicano/a culture, the first three stages characterize the life of the Latino/a who is self-loathing (stage 1), or a Chicano/a nationalist (stage 2), or is moving toward a border identity in which it is understood that border dwellers on both sides of the border have more in common with each other than with those in other regions of in either the United States or Mexico (stage 3). It is the fourth and fifth stages and that are currently dominant in the border region and that is gaining currency in the Chicana community. Biethnicity is what Anzaldúa describes as the new *mestiza* in *Borderlands*. The new *mestiza* is able to embrace the multiethnicity of the Chicano, that is, the indigenous, the African, and the European. As the border region begins to see itself in relation to the rest of the world, and as the Chicana influence on Chicano culture becomes hegemonic, an international perspective is replacing a provincial one in border cities, and a Chicana nationalism is replacing the Chicano nationalism of the 1960s. Border artists and writers are leading the way towards the sixth stage as they continue to forge links between Chicano/as and Palestinians, Chicano/as and Eastern European ethnic minorities, and feminists in Europe, Asia, Latin America and Africa. Schema such as this one devalue nationalism and see it as a stage in a progression towards internationalism. An alternative view is that the distinction between regional and international is itself being undermined in the era of globalization. Although Banks does not discuss the commodification of subjectivity directly, the proposed stages of ethnicity could be seen to mitigate against the tendency of capital to forge commodified subjectivities. In multicultural classrooms, such issues could be discussed without the imposition of a single perspective. At the university level, alternatives to Keynesian economics such as the work of Negri could be taught.

The multicultural classroom is not the norm in English departments at the university level. For the most part, assessment remains restricted to a punitive grading system that is harmful to all students, but particularly bilingual and bicultural students. Grammar and spelling errors become the teacher's justification for low grades for bilingual and bicultural students, despite the content of student work. Despite research done in linguistics about the cultural specificity of narrative structure, over twenty years of discussions about Derridean critiques of logocentrism, and critiques of assessment, the Cartesian five-paragraph essay remains the model in English courses. James A. Berlin (1993) argues that English studies should be reconfigured as Cultural Studies, and that cultural literacy should be the new goal. Eurocentric, middle-class models function even in prestigious creative writing environments, such as the Iowa Writer's Workshop, as Cisneros tells us with regard to her decision to write *The House on Mango Street.*

In his analysis of English Studies, Berlin notes that the major site for literacy teaching is the field of English, and that the field of English is in crisis. He refers to the work of Gerald Graff (1979) in which Graff argues that literary studies in the United States value the literary text and devalue the nonliterary text. Berlin points out that the nonliterary text is linked to the discourse of rhetoric, and more specifically, of science and politics. From the perspective of literacy in border regions, we can see the problem with restricting ourselves to literary studies as the proper or effective site for literacy teaching, and we can see why bilingual education is constantly under attack. By definition, bilingual education is located within the discourse of politics. As Deleuze and Guattari argue in *Kafka* (1986), for the deterritorialized subject, everything is political.

The teacher of literature to bilingual students must face the hostility or indifference of the field of English, which would prefer to ignore the discourses of rhetoric and politics and restrict itself to literary studies narrowly defined. Berlin's solution to this is to call on English to redefine itself as cultural studies. For the bilingual educator, this is a promising strategy. Berlin also refers to the work of Robert Scholes (1985), who argues that in literature departments, text interpretation is privileged over text production. Although Berlin applauds Scholes's attention to the deconstructing of binary oppositions within literature departments such as sacred and profane texts, the priestly class and the menial class, and "beauty and truth utilitarian and commonplace," he wants to go further (Berlin, 256). First, he explains the context of the status quo:

> The abhorrence of the rhetorical, of political and scientific texts, in English studies does far more than create a permanent underclass of department members at the college level whose putative role is the remediation of the poorly prepared. More importantly, it serves to exclude from the ranks of the privileged managerial class those students not socialized from birth in the ways of the aesthetic response, doing so by its influence on the materials and

methods of reading and writing required for success in secondary schools, college admission tests, and the colleges themselves (Berlin 1993, 257).

If Anglo children are excluded by virtue of their not belonging to the managerial class, we can see how bilingual and bicultural children suffer even more from the way in which English departments define literature and literacy. At the same time, we see that a strategic point at which to enter these debates in universities is at the level of the lowly composition teacher in the rhetoric department. Berlin's plans for (1) undermining the hierarchy that underestimates composition/rhetoric students and teachers and literature students and teachers and (2) calling for the redefinition of English departments as cultural studies departments are laudable. Unfortunately, without bilingual and bicultural teachers and students working together to bring non-Anglo middle-class cultural knowledge into the university, these measures will be insufficient. Furthermore, the majority Anglo population in both English and rhetoric programs will have to make a conscious effort to become more knowledgeable about other cultures and social classes. Those in border regions should attempt to borderize themselves by becoming bilingual and bicultural.

The theoretical approach in the following discussion will draw heavily on the work of McLaren in *Schooling as a Ritual Performance* (1986). Like the ritual, biculturalism does not express or represent; there is nothing outside the ritual. The ritual articulates. Similarly, biculturalism articulates bicultural reality. This process goes beyond mere bilingualism. Furthermore, McLaren claims that ritual can help us to understand how students develop and preserve their identities. This is important, in our use of McLaren's claim, for two reasons: (1) both the teacher and the student can be given a context for developing reflexivity about cultural identity; (2) the transformative pedagogical theorist can examine the way in which nonwhite students are codified in the educational system.

McLaren makes a distinction between three states that are characterized by different kinds of rituals: the student state, the sanctity state, and the street corner state. I want to discuss his model in relation to Spinoza's pleasant encounters in the "good" City. For Spinoza, blessedness can only take place in sociality. I want to substitute Spinoza's blessedness for McLaren's sanctity. McLaren's category of sanctity is complex in that it describes a set of religious rituals that are institutionalized and which have the function of imposing an identity: "We are Catholic." Only occasionally does it consist of a spiritual sense:

"Ideally, students in the sanctity state are filled with a realization of something greater beyond themselves which cannot be explained in rational terms" (McLaren 1986, 90). Being herded into a room for prayers is not sociality in Spinoza's sense. I want to conceive of a good classroom in which there could be a blurring of the distinction between the three states. Rather than a strict division between the inside of school and the outside of the street corner, in which the teacher reprimanded students with comments about waiting until after class to engage in certain activities, the camaraderie of the street corner could be combined with group learning in the classroom. McLaren points out that for well-behaved students, there is a willingness to work in groups, but this is a sociality that is based on being well-behaved in the student state. In Spinoza's pleasant encounter, elements of the sanctity state and the street corner state are combined. Some elements are not present in Spinoza's model, such as the violence which sometimes occurs in the street corner state. If, as McLaren claims, ritual can provide an opportunity for students to examine how their images are codified and maintained in the social order, then perhaps a combined state in which rituals from school, sanctity and street corner states could not only provide this discourse for reflexivity but also the possibility for Spinoza's pleasant encounter rather than violent confrontation, and by extension, a redefinition of the subject, the community and the state.

I have experienced how a community can calm a violent, disruptive person. At a pow-wow at the Barona reservation in San Diego, an inebriated Native American stumbled into the central area in which dances and rituals were being performed. He was loud and disruptive and showed no signs of leaving. I was filming the pow-wow, and I assumed that security persons would come and take care of the situation. Instead, the person leading the ceremony stopped everything and addressed this individual over the microphone. He told him that everyone there loved him and knew that he was in pain. Very calmly, he reminded the man of the importance of the pow-wow and of the community. The man slowly left the stage area and returned to the bleachers. He had not been humiliated and there had been no negative judgment made.

I want to describe a community in which McLaren's three states coexist and there is an attempt to bring the resources of the community into the classroom. Perkins Elementary School is located next to the historic Chicano Park in Barrio Logan in San Diego. The park is the site of political rallies, Day of the Dead celebrations, and rituals of *conchero* dancers which include Native American rituals such as the burning of sage. It contains murals that have now become internationally known. Street corner culture exists around the school, and includes workers eating lunch together as well as the kind of street corner culture McLaren describes, in part because Barrio Logan is an old Latino neighborhood that has been divided by freeways. Therefore, popular restaurants, industry and residences are all crowded together. The school is an elementary school, and due to parental involvement and a very hands-on approach of the principal and vice-principal and parental involvement, there is not the problem with violence in or around the school described by McLaren. Mothers, grandmothers, aunts, and sometimes fathers and grandfathers walk their children and other neighbor children to school and walk them home. Just as McLaren does not want to romanticize the street corner state, I do not want to romanticize the pow-wow as a panacea for all problems on reservations or the *barrio* as a model community. Problems on reservations of alcoholism, suicide, diabetes, unemployment, and education, as well as others, are well documented. Students in the *barrio* are subject to noxious fumes. There are toxic dumpsites. At night, and sometimes even during the day, there is violence. Although Perkins is a magnet school, many parents are unaware of the resources of the school and are confused about and resentful towards the GATE program. Some, frustrated, would rather send their children to wealthier neighborhoods if they could, where they believe their children would get a better education. There is social resentment against lighter-skinned Latino students. Some parents criticize activist parents as "having nothing better to do with their lives than go to meetings" and use after-school study programs as baby-sitting rather than as an opportunity to create a more supportive educational environment for their children. On the part of some parents, there is a suspicion towards "outsiders," that is, parents who do not live in the immediate neighborhood within walking distance of the school. Nevertheless, there is a strong sense of community surrounding the school; a block from the school there is a community health clinic. *Comadres* sell snacks and *monitas* across the street from the school, or, on special days, on the playground. Over twenty years of activism in the neighborhood gives the school advantages not found elsewhere; for example, a parent meeting is able to attract the director of the state budget committee, a council person, and a member of the school board, and the vice-principal is from the neighborhood and quotes Paulo Freire in meetings with parents. Yet, a recent court ruling gave polluters the right to sue the school district and the environmentalists. Quite rightly, the environmentalists argued that the suit brought against them was merely a vicious tactic to silence them. Children continue to cough, wheeze, get stomachaches and headaches and suffer other effects of the toxins that surround them.[3]

The knowledge within the community around the school is a valuable resource for the multicultural classroom. Freire proposes a pedagogy that "starts from the knowledge the learner brings to school" (1993, 77). In the case of the bilingual/bicultural student, this is the knowledge of the nondominant culture. This kind of pedagogy is supported by McLaren (1994) who refers to a study by Luis Moll (1992) at the University of Arizona in which researchers searched for "funds of knowledge" in families in a predominantly Mexican, working-class community. They wanted to know how knowledge is constructed "within the family dwelling . . . in terms of job sharing, and between the families . . . Moll wanted to understand the kind of pedagogy employed by parents, as well as by uncles, aunts and community leaders. Parents and relatives were knowledgeable in a variety of areas including soil cultivation, planting, water distribution and management, animal husbandry, veterinary medicine, ranch economy, auto mechanics, carpentry, masonry, electrical wiring, fencing, herbal cures, midwifery, and first aid" (McLaren 1994, 152). These are the "funds of knowledge" are part of the life experience which the bicultural/bilingual student brings to school. For Freire, the role of the educator should be to establish a dialogic model with the student rather than a banking model in which the educator deposits knowledge. The implications of this belief for bilingual education are clear: the bilingual teacher does better to establish a dialogic model in the classroom in which the knowledge the student has, of language and of the world, is valued, rather than to merely deposit linguistic knowledge about the target language.

A study that has grown out of Luis Moll's work is the establishment of an *instituto familiar* at Carr Middle School in Southern California, as discussed by Carmen Zuñiga and Sylvia Alatorre Alva (1995). They point out that the involvement of parents in schools is "particularly important for immigrant parents because it provides a way to close the cultural and linguistic gap that commonly exists, especially as adolescents become increasingly absorbed into the cultural norms and expectations of the dominant society" (7). Barrio Logan Elementary Institute (BLEI) parents in Barrio Logan in San Diego are painfully aware of this gap. Some avoid BLEI activities because they do not wish to be judged as "uneducated" in a context which focuses on getting their children into college.

At the university level, an innovative project at State University has begun in the last year that will bring together scholars and members of the community in the humanities and the sciences to develop a multicultural curriculum. This group hopes to address, among other concerns, the issue of the very small number of Native American students at the university. An attempt is being made to include the aspect of ritual in the organization of the group, which will include retreats. There will also be an attempt to educate the educators through reading materials together and viewing videotapes about multicultural and other related programs.

A major problem for bilingual and bicultural students at the K–12 level is the "push out" rate, often misconstrued as the "drop-out" rate. I will argue, following Freire, that it is the structure of educational institutions, not the decisions of individual students, that result in the "drop-out" rate. Furthermore, as Paul Willis (1981) has shown in relation to students in England, and as many teachers in the Latino community have observed, the decision to pursue other avenues than higher education is not a passive one; rather, it is a rejection of a system that students find to be cynical and hypocritical.

In the San Diego-Tijuana border region, there are many contradictory attitudes and social forces surrounding the education of bicultural and bilingual students. Even educators who have studied the region do not agree about the causes of the attrition problem. Some blame parents while others blame racism. Teachers and parents are often pitted against each other, each feeling that the other does not understand or care. Administrators, even well-meaning ones, often have to engage in triage decisions that disrupt the community, family-based lives of bilingual and bicultural students, as children as young as fifth graders are bussed to schools outside of their communities due to overcrowding. One of the most publicized concerns is the so-called drop-out rate.

In *Pedagogy of the City*, Freire explains the concept of the drop-out in Brazil

> The Brazilian poor children do not drop out of school; they don't leave school because they want to. The Brazilian poor children are expelled from school

not, obviously, because this or that teacher, for a reason of pure personal antipathy, expels these students or flunks them. It is the very structures of society that push students out: obstacles for the children of subordinate classes to come to school (1993, 30).

The situation of being "pushed out" also applies to Latino/a students in California. The graduation rate from high school is generally believed to be around sixty-two percent for Mexican-American students, although figures vary. Another aspect of the educational system that pushes students out is the ethnic breakdown of students and teachers. While "most educators and minority parents agree on the need for teachers who mirror the colors and cultures of their students," in San Diego Country, "[t]here are 72 minority students for every minority teacher" (Devise 1997 A1, 14). The teacher, regardless of ethnic background, in the bicultural and bilingual classroom, regardless of ethnic background, is in a position to resist these structures, despite the overwhelming statistical imbalances.

One way of resisting the structures is for the teacher to examine his or her attitudes toward the language of bilingual students and towards the task of teaching "literate discourse styles to all of their students" (Delpit 1995, 152).[4] Arguing against critics from the right, Freire's comments about the speech patterns of poor Brazilian students also apply to bilingual students:

I have never said or written . . . that poor children should not learn the "standard pattern." For that it is necessary that they feel their identity respected and that they not feel inferior for speaking differently. . . . it is necessary that, as they exercise their right to learn the standard patterns, they realize that they should do it not because their language is ugly or inferior, but because by mastering the so-called standard patterns they become empowered to fight for the necessary reinvention of the world (1993, 41–42).

In terms of the debates surrounding bilingualism, this is the view that bilingual education is not meant to keep a child speaking only Spanish, but to ensure that the child will learn English. In her research in Papua New Guinea, Delpit found that children who were allowed to be educated in their first language, or *tok ples*, in pre-school, or *Vilis Tokples Pri-Skul*, learned English better than students educated only in English (1995, 88). Challenging the views of progressive teachers, Delpit writes of a "certain sense of powerlessness and paralysis among many sensitive and well-meaning educators" who "question whether they are acting as agents of oppression by insisting that students who are not already a part of the 'mainstream' learn that discourse. Delpit points out that "students and parents of color" and progressive teachers often find themselves on opposite sides of the bilingual debate and the skills/process debate in the teaching of writing (1995, 152). Regarding bilingual education, parents often want the emphasis to be on English rather than Spanish. This is analogous to Delpit's observation that parents of African-American children want their children to learn standard English. In terms of the method of teaching, progressive teachers favor process while African-American parents and teachers expects skills. Although the audiences being addressed by Freire and Delpit are very different, with Freire often justifying a progressive viewpoint under attack by conservatives in Brazil, and while functioning in a position of political power, and Delpit mediating between primarily white, progressive educators, on one side, and African- American and Native American teachers, parents and students, on the other, they are proponents of a similar position. Both argue that students need to be prepared to function in their own environment, whether that be as children in Brazil from poor backgrounds or nonmiddle-class African-American backgrounds, as well as in the environment of the dominant discourse.

Two phenomena considered in this chapter, first, the valorizing, in the field of English, of the white subject, and second, the pushing out of non-Anglo, and particularly Latino/a, students are related to the logic of late capitalism in which the subject is selected, that is, produced and consumed. Within this system, there is no crisis of literacy; instead, the so-called literacy problem serves to obscure the privileging of the white subject. By attacking the double standard of bilingualism, elite and folk, and the distinction between rhetoric and literature in which politics and science are excluded from the purview of literature, we may begin to redefine bilingualism and literacy in order to: (1) create the optimal learning environment for culturally and linguistically diverse students; (2) ensure that teachers are trained in multiculturalism to function effectively in multicultural classrooms; (3) create rituals that help students to develop a discourse of reflexivity about their identities; and (4) value the knowledge in communities around schools and to create learning links with those communities.

Notes

1. This situation is complicated by the economic factor, that schools receive funding for Spanish-speaking (Limited English Proficiency) students. There are many problems that currently plague the school system in California with regard to LEP students, including: 1) many Latino children need extra help and do not receive it; and 2) some Latino children are put into these LEP programs whether they need them or not.

2. For more information on Native American students in the classroom see Vine Deloria, Jr., *Indian Education in America*. Boulder: American Science and Engineering Society, 1991.

3. I recently completed a project that deals with ecological issues. The project included members of the Computer Club at Perkins Elementary School in San Diego and students from the Oaxacan community in Tijuana under the auspices of the CECUT (Centro Cultural de Tijuana) A performance character I created, based on the photographer Tina Modotti, Ecotina, helps the children in Barrio Logan locate a company that has been dumping toxic waste at the San Diego Zoo and in Barrio Logan. Because the children have access to computers, the images have been scanned and the book is available both as a print out and in hypermedia with sound. A student reads the story in both languages and it is also available on videotape. The rationale for the performance character is that the character, inspired by Super Barrio in Mexico City, has superpowers and can help the children improve social conditions. When I presented the project to the Perkins students, they excitedly revealed that their parents worked in the polluting companies, that they had heard stories about pollution from family members, and that they had suffered health problems as well. One company, a school sponsor and a major polluter, happened to be leading an assembly while we met. That company donated notebooks, with their logo, to all of the students. A student suggested that the notebooks be boycotted and that we proceed to the auditorium to protest the presence of the company on the campus. Articles continue to appear in *The San Diego Union-Tribune* at the time of this writing regarding the pollution in Barrio Logan. Just recently, after a five-year struggle, parents in Barrio Logan achieved a victory in their struggle to protect their children from toxins when the Port of San Diego agreed to stop spraying fruit with methyl bromide.

4. Delpit's book is extremely important for educators, particularly progressive white educators, in the border region because she questions widely accepted beliefs and her examples make a link between the bilingual classroom of Spanish-English speakers and the multicultural classroom of Euroamerican and African–American students. Her interviews and classroom examples, especially those from the Native American community in Alaska, are very sugges-

tive for educators in the Latino community. For example, the strong influence of Native American culture and values in the Chicano, and especially the Chicana community, give her examples a power that is even stronger in the Chicano/a community than in the African-American community that is the focus of her book. Furthermore, Latino parents in the borderlands, like the parents in Papua New Guinea, are concerned about the loss of traditional culture; however, like African-American parents with regard to standard English, they fear that if their children do not learn English well, they will not succeed. Her suggestion that ethnographies could be done of various writing projects is a challenge to scholars in cultural studies.

Chapter 4

The Marketing of Ethnic Studies, Attacks on Affirmative Action, and the Obfuscation of "Whiteness"

In this chapter, I want to examine how the marketing of ethnic studies may serve to obscure the privileges of whites. Ethnic studies departments have been formed in order to consolidate the issues surrounding ethnicity and privilege and to isolate them into one more-easily-controlled environment.[1] However, this move has not been accompanied by a creation of Euroamerican studies departments. Faculty members agreeing to teach in these departments often do so not because they agree with the concept of ethnic studies, but because they fear that the alternative is even worse, that is, the disbanding of certain departments altogether. The context for this reorganization of departments in universities is the continuing assault on affirmative action. The attacks on affirmative action serve as a diversionary tactic to take attention away from the affirmative action that white males have always had. Light-skinned students, who call themselves white, do not usually specify what they mean by the term. If white is defined as privileged, then perhaps WASP would be more accurate. If it is a skin color, then it must be problematized in relation to Euroamerican, because that term does not include white Russians and others. The avoidance of these complexities serves to obscure the privileges of whites in power positions. Even some progressive educators, as Lisa Delpit points out in *Other People's Children*, need to reconsider the phrase: "I don't see color, I only see children" (1995, 177). In Delpit's view, the message given to the child is that color is something negative.

In the dialogue between Paulo Freire and Donaldo Macedo, Macedo writes:

If it were not for the amnesia prevalent within U.S. Society, it would be very easy to understand that the present cruel and frontal attack on affirmative action, immigrants, and unwed mothers is a mere continuation of a historical context where Blacks were "scientifically" relegated to a subhuman existence which, in turn, justified the irrationality of their alienating reality as slaves (1992, 423).

Despite the "white anger" that emerges from the view that "indeed, if any discrimination exists in America, it is racism toward Whites themselves," that is, despite the inability of some whites to perceive their privileges, white privileges have remained in place (Kincheloe, Steinberg and Gresson 1996, 25). The marketing of ethnic studies is a way to take away resources and political power from specific departments, such as African-American studies and Mexican-American studies, under the guise of creating a new department, Ethnic studies.

First, I will argue that the debates forming the backdrop of the formation of ethnic studies departments are really about (1) responsibility for the current economic situation, which, and here I agree with many of the critics in *Measured Lies*, is caused by corporate flight and the continued focus on the creation of 'favorable business climates,'; and (2) the canon, and the organization of knowledge (Spivak 1993). As Hardt and Negri argue, the multitude must be "autonomous producers of wealth, knowledge, and cooperation" (1994, 312).

Second, I will draw an analogy between the situation of the feminist postcolonial critic described by Nalini Natarajan (1994) and by Gayatri Spivak (1988) and that of the Chicana lesbian and the woman immigrant in order to look at the issues being discussed in a global context. In Europe, ethnic minorities are used as political pawns by all countries; the attacks on affirmative action in this country are not dissimilar in that members of both political parties are deceitful and self-serving with regard to the civil rights of nonwhite citizens. I want to discuss this problem from a border perspective informed by arguments of postcolonial and postmodernist critics. In *Scattered Hegemonies*'s discussion of nationalism, the poignant situation of the feminist postcolonial critic can be found.

Third, I will look at attacks on affirmative action, specifically those in recent legislation and in Richard J. Herrnstein and Charles Murray's *The Bell Curve* (1994). Many critics in *Measured Lies*, a collection of essays written in response to *The Bell Curve*, point out how affirmative action, the Civil Rights Movement and a democratic function of education are either direct or indirect targets of Hernstein and

Murray's book. Many of the descriptions of the criminalization of the young African-American male are discussed by Gutiérrez-Jones (1995). I will look at magnet schools because they pose a problem for the philosophical assumptions of *The Bell Curve*: They deconstruct the binary opposition white-intelligent/nonwhite-substandard intelligence because they get "cream" from all ethnic groups in the culture.

Fourth, drawing on the analysis made by Spivak of the canon debates, I will consider possible responses to these attacks, as those in Chicano studies, African-American studies and other ethnic studies departments attempt to continue to democratize the classroom. I will argue for a feminist component in possible responses and for the need to respond in a way in which there is a defense of affirmative action, the gains of the Civil Rights movement and the democratic function of education. Rather than supporting or attacking the decision to participate in ethnic studies departments, I will call for educators to analyze individual situations in the terms discussed above.

In the era of late capitalism, wealth and knowledge are not distributed in an equitable manner. Aronowitz contextualizes the discussion of this unequal distribution when interviewed by Shirley Steinberg. He argues that the view that blacks are inferior resurfaces cyclically because it is a cultural, not a scientific phenomenon. Corporate flight and the creation of a "favorable business climates" are the real causes of the current economic situation, despite the fact that affirmative action and undocumented workers are scapegoated. Although a college education is no guarantee of a job, applicants may be told that the reason they are being rejected is because they do not have a college degree. Thus, the educational system is important as a strategic site; it issues the passports to the corporate world.

Howard Winant (1977) broadens this discussion by offering several useful categories that organize the political positions in the current debates concerning racism: the far right, the new right, the neoconservative, the neoliberal and the abolitionist. The most blatant and theatrical attacks on immigration and bilingual education are linked to the far right, which is very strong in San Diego; the far right has been consistently attacked by Chicano/a activists and artists. Organizations of the far right in San Diego include the White Aryan Resistance, which has written hate mail to human rights activist Roberto Martínez. One of the letters was in turn used in an art exhibition by the Chicana/Mexican/Anglo feminist collective Las Comadres in the late 1980s. In 1996 and 1997, an African-American professor at Cal

State San Marcos was singled out for persecution by the far right. A more difficult line of defense by progressives has been in the university classroom, where neoconservative views are very strong among students. The neoconservatives want to go 'beyond race.' Winant writes: "Neo-conservative discourse seeks to preserve white advantages through denial of racial difference " (1977, 11). Here we see one example of the obfuscation of whiteness. It is here that I want to look at the move to redesign departments such as African-American Studies and Chicano studies into ethnic studies and to the discussion of the canon. Winant continues: "Neoliberal discourse seeks to limit white advantages through denial of racial differences." This sounds similar to neoconservative discourse, but Winant clarifies the position. "It seeks systematically to narrow the differences which divide working and middle-class people as a strategy for improving 'life-chances' of minorities, who are disproportionately poor" (1997, 14). Winant characterizes this project as "social democratic, focused on social structure (as opposed to cultural representation a la the various right-wing racial projects), and somewhat class reductionist in its approach to race (1997, 14). From the perspective of the Chicano/a activists in the border region, the neoliberal viewpoint underemphasizes the issue of racism. Winant's critique of this viewpoint, that it is inadequate in responding to the problem of residential segregation and criminal justice, is quite relevant to San Diego and the West Coast. The neoliberal viewpoint is present in the curriculum of bilingual educators, who are taught to expose their students from poor backgrounds to middle-class culture in order to help them to become upwardly mobile. Winant also attacks the neoliberal viewpoint because it does not challenge the white "willingness to receive a 'psychological wage,' which amounts to a tangible benefit acquired at the expense of nonwhites" (1997, 16). Finally, Winant discusses the abolitionist project and quotes Roediger (1991):

> It is not merely that whiteness is oppressive and false; it is that whiteness is nothing but oppressive and false . . . It is the empty and terrifying attempt to build an identity based on what one isn't and on whom one can hold back (quoted in Winant 1997, 17).

Two strategies that have been used to insure that knowledge will not be distributed in an equitable manner are attacks on affirmative action and attacks on civil rights. One gain of the civil rights movement was desegregation; translated into the curriculum, desegregation demands the revising of the canon. Spivak, discussing the revision of the canon, makes the point that there can be "no general theory of canons" an that "the matter of the literary canon is in fact a political matter; securing authority" (1993, 270–271). Spivak lists the "others" most often invoked in discussions of revisions of the canon: "women, women of color, gays, lesbians; Afro-America; immigrant literature; literature of ethnicity; working-class literature; working-class women; non-Western literature; and, in peculiar companionship, something called 'theory'" (1993, 272). She proposes "yoking" English with other disciplines, such as anthropology and African studies (277). Spivak insists on a language requirement so that there is not a creation of a literary canon of Third World literature in translation that itself constitutes a new form of orientalism (1977, 277). Although she does not discuss the attacks on attempts to open the canon, it is well documented that attempts to open the canon have been surrounded by controversy. One of the more well-known controversies was that surrounding the Western civilization course at Stanford. Spivak's suggestion that English attach itself other disciplines seems to offer an alternative to collapsing many "ethnic" departments into ethnic studies.

Both affirmative action and the organization of Chicano studies as a field are also related to the division of knowledge in the university as a whole, that is, ultimately, to canon debates in English in relation to Chicano/a texts. Karen Lunt (1996) argues that Chicana writers Cisneros and Anzaldúa should be included in the realm of what is considered American literature. As a political strategy, some Chicano Studies scholars might take the position that it is important to protect Chicano Studies and simultaneously, fight to open the canon in English departments to include Chicano/a writers. Lunt's essay suggests that in Anzaldúa's case, gender issues take the work outside of a traditional Chicano perspective, and therefore the work can benefit by being explored from a feminist perspective in American literature. She also suggests that Cisneros be studied in American literature; she notes that Cisneros did not consider herself to be a Latina until 1976, when she began to renegotiate her cultural identity as the Iowa Workshop. It was the Native American writer Joy Harjo who helped her to identify her own voice.

One way to question the canon is to to examine the work of writers who are positioned at the edges of it. Two writers, Gloria Anzaldúa and Sandra Cisneros, are useful examples of writers whose work cannot be restricted to traditional Chicano Studies or Mexican-American studies departments; yet they are not part of the American literature canon. Many Chicana scholars and a few Chicano scholars are dealing with gender issues that make it possible to discuss these writers, including Tey Diana Rebolledo (1995), Ana Castillo (1995) and Gutiérrez-Jones (1995).

Now, I will draw an analogy between the feminist postcolonial situation and that of the Chicana lesbian and the woman immigrant. In her essay "Women, Nation and Narration in *Midnight's Children*," in *Scattered Hegemonies* (1994), Nalini Natarajan explains how the imaginary of India, the shape of a nation in the minds of citizens divided by caste, region, class, religion and language, is played out on the body of the woman. Because English is the "official" language, but not everyone has access to literacy or the press, it is the film and not the written word that unites the nation. Ironically, although the image of India is the Hindu mother, it is a Moslem actress who played the role in the film that galvanized this image. This violence against the Moslem, difference, and woman in her own right rather than as she is useful in order to create a national identity, can be supported on the basis of the need to develop a national consciousness against British imperialism, but it is problematic. It obscures Hindu hegemony. At the moment, in the United States, several sorts of elisions for the sake of identity are taking place: (1) attacks on affirmative action now threaten to dismantle it altogether, all in the name of "equality"; (2) some Chicano studies (and African-American studies, Native American studies and Asian American studies) are agreeing to be absorbed into ethnic studies departments; (3) some Chicano studies departments, along with other departments, continue to fight being absorbed. In the first case, there is an attempt to obscure the privilege of whites. In the second, the very name, ethnic studies, suggests that whites come from an origin that is pure and was never tainted by "ethnicity." From a border perspective, sensitive to gender concerns, it must be asked how Chicanas, for example, will or have fared in these different scenarios. Chicano nationalism has, as nationalism in India has, used the woman as a way to solidify identity. This resulted in a silencing of difference, as in the case of the Chicana lesbian.

In India, film has been able to galvanize Indian identity even for the nonliterate. In the United States, images of African-Americans and Latinos are negative stereotypes of drug-dealers and gang members. The criminalization of the African-American male, described by several critics in Kincheloe, Steinberg and Gresson (1996), reverberates in the descriptions by Gutiérrez-Jones (1995) of the criminalization of the Latino. What Indian film was able to establish was an alternative to a British, colonial norm. Although it might be argued that there is an attempt to do this in some rap music in the United States, the stereotypes that also occur in rap would undermine this viewpoint. The problem, then, for the young African-American and Latino male, for example, is that he is rejected as inferior to the white norm in the culture as a whole and in the school system.

One response to the unequal distribution of knowledge, if not wealth, and to racism, has been affirmative action in educational institutions. Recent legislation in California has succeeded in dismantling affirmative action in the elite University of California system. In order to show the direct link between Herrnstein and Murray's *The Bell Curve* and border cultural and political concerns, I turn to Kincheloe and Steinberg's discussion of Proposition 187:

> The Pioneer Fund is an exciting place to be in the 1990s with the election of legislators who support many of the organization's views and who turn to it for pertinent information on pending legislation. Fund director Harry Weyner has endorsed the brilliance of *The Bell Curve*, as well he should. A sizable number of the sources utilized by Herrnstein and Murray were produced by Pioneer Fund recipients. Embedded in right-wing political circles, the Pioneer Fund's most favored political organization is the Federation of American Immigration Reform (FAIR). It was this organization that helped California Governor Pete Wilson formulate support for Proposition 187 (1996 38–9).

A more abstract, but equally significant link to border concerns can be found in the wonderfully ludic essay by Alan Shelton, "The Ape's IQ," in which he approaches *The Bell Curve* in relation to Kafka's story "A Report to the Academy:"

> Kafka's story is part of a genre that is common enough along the borders where cultures meet, particularly when that context is marked by racism and violence. *The Bell Curve* is never far away from that genre itself in the way the borders are dramatized between an essentially white affluent class and everyone else. (94)

This describes the San Diego-Tijuana border quite accurately.

Now I will look at attacks on affirmative action, including Herrnstein and Murray's *The Bell Curve*. Many critics in *Measured Lies* point out how affirmative action, the Civil Rights Movement and a democratic function of education are either direct or indirect targets of the book. As Kincheloe, Steinberg and Gresson explain in "Who Says It

Can't Happen Here," *The Bell Curve* reduces the problems in our culture today to the inclusion of "the cream" from all strata of society. This reduction, according to their argument, leaves U.S. society with an uneducated, unintelligent population that is responsible for crime, drug use, and other types of immoral behavior. Desegregation takes many forms, one of which has been bussing to magnet schools. Magnet schools create a dilemma for Herrnstein and Murray. On the one hand, they would fall into Herrnstein and Murray's "cream" theory, because bussing bright students from the middle class to well-funded magnet schools, and including non-Anglo children from poorer class backgrounds in magnet schools, is a way in which "gifted" students are identified from all strata of society. However, a logical extension of the arguments of *The Bell Curve* would lead the reader to attack magnet schools as part of affirmative action. In fact, the magnet concept is the unpleasant meeting ground of neoconservative discourse and neoliberal discourse. The magnet concept does attack residential segregation, by providing bussing, which links it to the goals of progressive Chicano/a activists. It seeks to improve the "life chances," of students, in part through the identification of gifted and talented children regardless of race, and also by creating schools with specific emphases, such as foreign languages, performing arts, and marine biology . Both Anglo and non-Anglo children are encouraged to participate in the magnet program. Due to the complex and contradictory underlying philosophical assumptions of the magnet program, it overlaps with both neo-conservative and neo-liberal discourse and it is a target of the far right. The GATE program, part of the Magnet schools, shares one underlying assumption with *The Bell Curve*, that is, the privileging of a high IQ and the belief in the IQ test.

Affirmative action is also part of desegregation, so, under the guise of science, *The Bell Curve* can attack this very significant outgrowth of the Civil Rights movement and the New Left without doing so directly. Kincheloe, Steinberg and Gresson report that Herrnstein made a boast before he died that *The Bell Curve* would "destroy racially preferential admissions in the university" (1996, 12). The tragic irony of all of this is that even though the statistics presented in the book present the exact opposite of their case for a high correlation between IQ and job performance, as shown by Richard Cary in his essay "IQ as Commodity" (1996), this will get past readers not trained in statistics.

The brilliance of the strategy of Hernnstein and Murray is that their targets are hit at a subliminal level. As Kincheloe and Steinberg "hidden theoretical assumptions about Herrnstein and Murray's science are consumed unknowingly by readers" (1996, 7). The backdrop of Herrnstein and Murray's performance is their argument about the "creaming" of the talented, but the focus of the book, evidenced by how many times it is repeated, is the vilification of some "unintelligent," "immoral" part of the population that threatens to bring down the whole society.

The "creaming" of the talented is also a goal of the magnet program. Many of Kincheloe and Steinberg's points in their essay "Who Said It Can't Happen Here" (1996) overlap with those I am making here. I want to clarify one point that may appear to contradict their views. They discuss tracking, and I want to distinguish tracking from the magnet system as it functions in the San Diego Unified School District. They point to studies that show that "tracking holds harmful consequences for low IQ students and the school in general, as (contrary to the conventional wisdom) it undermines the achievement of lower track students without improving upper-track students' performance (Oakes 1985; Grubb et. al., 1991; Beck 1991)" (Kincheloe and Steinberg 1996, 11).[2] Unlike tracking, which often places middle-class children in the highest tracks and poorer children in the lower tracks, the magnet system attempts to include children from all socioeconomic and ethnic backgrounds. However, the result is often the same. In my son's second-grade seminar class, all except one student were middle or upper-middle class. One child lived in low-income housing one block from the school. Working-class and poor children were not by any means represented in this group of students. One child, whose parents lived in the wealthy suburb of La Jolla, was brought to school every day in the family car, a late model Jaguar.

As applied in San Diego, the magnet school concept includes "mixing," a part of the day in which cluster and seminar students interact with students in the rest of the school. The entire school benefits, at least theoretically. In practice, I have seen this to be the case in the classroom, although I have heard that there are abuses of this system at some schools. However, on the playground, at least from my observations of elementary schools, the situation is quite different. If a magnet school does not have a commitment to conflict resolution, and most do not, and if the playground is overcrowded and undersupervised, and most are, fights become the norm. Racial and class resentments resonate in violent dodge ball games, where there is at least some interaction, or in complete segregation, as in sitting at separate tables at lunch. As positive an experience as the magnet schools may provide for some children, particularly "the gifted," Ladislaus Semali's critique is part of the backdrop against which any particular magnet program must be judged:

> I heard ABC announce the results of research by Professor Mary Frasier at the University of Georgia who has challenged the whole idea of 'giftedness' in the state's schools. Typically, only about 1% of school-age students are reckoned as 'gifted.' Nationwide, there are about 2 to 3% of 'gifted' students of any race. In Atlanta, Georgia, Professor Frasier found that students must have an IQ score of 130 to qualify as 'gifted.' In this category about 17 percent were minorities and 26 percent were white. These discrepancies led Frasier to examine closely IQ scores, which are by and large believed to be used as a cover for segregation. Besides, many students who would have qualified as "gifted" are never tested (1995, 165).

Kincheloe, Steinberg and Tippins discuss IQ, the notion of "gifted" and the problems with the whole idea of genius in their book *The Stigma of Genius* (1992).

In San Diego, the gifted and talented program includes students on the basis of intellectual ability, creative ability, specific academic ability, leadership ability, high achievement, and visual and performing arts talent. The breadth of the criteria, which go beyond intellectual ability alone, reflects legislation which became effective in 1989. The state of California defines the gifted as within the top two percent of students, reflected in legislation in 1961. In San Diego, research begun in 1948 on the top one-half of one per cent of the student population found that "only half were doing as well in their classes as pupils with average ability and approximately half of them had social adjustment problems of some severity" (*Gifted and Talented Program* n.d., 5). I know that in the early 1960s, I was in some kind of "gifted" program but I have no idea which one; many of the students in the program with me, especially in elementary school, definitely had "social adjustment problems," and I remember that jokes by other students were made about us and about Special Ed students. As students in a third-fourth grade combination class, we were definitely nerds: we refused to say the flag salute, talked about UFOs and read *The Hobbit* series. However, as a girl within this group, and because I was from a very dysfunctional family, I felt like an outsider even with these outsiders, and I was sure that they had placed me with these "smart" students by mistake.

My recent experience as a postgraduate fellow with teachers of Seminar students in the American Council of Learned Societies K–12

Curriculum Project in the context of a group of twenty K–12 teachers was quite frustrating at first. In a group of twenty teachers that supposedly represented the cultural and ethnic diversity of the district, there were no Latinos or Latinas, there was no interest in border issues, and there were racist stereotypes about Latina girls among the teachers in the group generally, without singling out Seminar teachers. Because the teachers knew that my ex-husband is Mexican and that I write about border issues, the room would get quiet when I entered during some of the conversations I overheard, but I heard enough to get the gist of the conversations. One teacher, who was African-American, was an exception, but she was not a GATE teacher. She was team-teaching with a Latina teacher at her school and included Chicano/a literature at the high school level in her curriculum plans. Another, a musician who had attended seminary before becoming a teacher, was also an exception. Although I learned a great deal from all of the teachers about multiple intelligence, small-group teaching, and many alternatives to the typical university lecture style, I noticed that these teachers in most cases did not have the cultural knowledge necessary to deal with non-Anglo students. The majority of them expected less of non-Anglo students and complained, sometimes bitterly, about the non-Anglo student populations in their schools.

Because of this experience, I was prepared for the worst when my bilingual son entered school. Although he is now enduring school, it continues to be a struggle. His kindergarten was under-funded and did not have a Spanish language immersion program. The school where he attended first and second grade was an excellent magnet school with a Spanish language immersion program but did not have seminar classes, and although he was put in an advanced fourth-grade logic class as a second grader, the school did not want him to skip any grades. Next, he attended his third school, where he learned to write essays in both Spanish and English and discovered computer culture through The Computer Club and the dedicated director of the computer lab. This school is located in Barrio Logan, the Latino neighborhood of San Diego. Unfortunately, this school has no experience yet with multicultural conflict resolution, in part because it is a 98 per cent Latino student body. Now, however, the ethnic population is shifting, and preparations such as the Latino and African-American Boy's Club are being made. Perkins Elementary faces tremendous challenges of health-threatening pollution, very little space, and the social problems of poor, isolated neighborhoods. At the time of this writing, playground conflicts are growing worse rather than improving. A visionary vice-principal is attempting to bring Freirean ideas to the school, but change creates resistance to change. Next year, my son will attend another seminar class, in an African-American neighborhood, with an emphasis on space exploration. Even more impressive than this emphasis and the computer lab is the focus on human relations and conflict resolution, which is supported by a full-time psychologist.

It is obvious to me that redlining, designation as "inner city" or "suburban," and community activism are all factors in the situation in which a parent, a child and a single school find themselves *vis-à-vis* the school district. When I lived in an upscale neighborhood, next to but not part of an old money neighborhood, my son attended the nearest elementary school. Because of the odd divisions in the district, this school received very little money. It could not even afford a PTA, and the principal, when I asked her about the lack of heat, said she had to choose between repairing leaks in the roof and heat. I had attended that school thirty years before, and I had received a very high-tech Sputnik child education. It appeared that the now torn curtains in the auditorium were the same ones that had been there when I attended. The principal at the school is highly respected, but her options were limited by the financial constrictions she faced. Just as I was about to give up all hope of my son receiving a good public education, my own economic situation changed drastically. I moved into the edge of the barrio, very close to downtown, in a redlined, economically depressed area. However, many activists live in this largely Latino but completely integrated neighborhood. There are, in a variety of combined identities, many gays, lesbians, bisexuals, artists, actors, musicians, teachers, city planners, and architects in this neighborhood, and even a circus made up of neighborhood kids who work with professionals. Through the combined efforts of a variety of coalitions that had formed in this neighborhood, there is a strong network of interested parents with whom I was able to keep in close contact. It is through the information I gather from these parents and support from the administrations at magnet schools that I have been able to negotiate the continuing changes of schools to meet the changing needs of my son.

The third school in my son's odyssey is one of the best schools in terms of technology in the district, and it is less than two miles from home. He has been able to attend a bilingual, bicultural after-school computer club. I was afraid that in order to be in the seminar class, a combined second through fourth, but his teacher is a native Spanish speaker and the class is taught bilingually throughout the day. However, in his fourth school, which he will begin next year, he will not be able to continue his bilingual emphasis.

After these experiences, first with the American Council of Learned Societies project and second with my son's saga, I was interested in some Venn diagram that I could use to explain what I had learned about schooling, segregation, magnet schools, and the GATE program in San Diego. I was especially impressed with some of the teachers I met at my son's second, third, and fourth schools. To date, I have found only one area of overlap: one of the teachers in the ACLS project, the musician I mentioned earlier, who is very interested in border culture and pedagogy, lives in my neighborhood. The magnet resource teacher at one of the schools had read the ACLS K–12 Curriculum Project report I had worked on, which I discovered quite by accident during a brief conversation while I turned in the exit form that allowed my son to change schools. Aside from these two teachers, I have had no contact at all with any of the ACLS project-related activities, people, bureaucracies, organizations, national meetings, or any other aspect of that three-year project. Somehow, the very thing that the ACLS was hoping could occur in the future is happening everyday in San Diego; there are truly dedicated, multicultural, bilingual, open-minded, experimental, creative teachers from the community working within the community. They are working, however, somehow, in a parallel reality. It is a reality in which the majority of San Diego teachers are removed from the everyday lives and communities of African-Americans, Latinos, and other non-Anglo students. Nevertheless, the fact that one teacher had read the report gave me hope that there was some link, no matter how tenuous, between these realities.

Having looked at affirmative action, specifically, magnet schools, at the K–12 level, I will now turn to affirmative action at the university level. I will consider possible responses to the attacks on affirmative action, as those in Chicano studies, African-American studies and other ethnic studies departments continue their struggle to democratize the classroom. Chicano/a scholars and activists are currently grappling with the situation in many universities in which Chicano studies departments are being absorbed into an ethnic studies department. I think that the question is not either Chicano studies or ethnic studies, but a multifaceted approach that responds to the historical trends and attacks from the Right considered above. Unlike English departments, which have not had to justify their existence each year to the same extent, Chicano studies departments must, therefore, continually stress the importance of affirmative action, the rights of farm workers, various political economic interactions between the U.S. and Mexico, from the Treaty of Guadalupe to the effects of North American Free Trade Agreement, hold education to its promise of what Aronowitz calls the "broad basis of equality." Educators are faced with unpleasant choices, to insist on separate departments and to refuse integration, which may mean ceasing to exist, to join ethnic studies departments willingly, or to take a critical stance towards integration into ethnic studies departments by negotiating as much as possible.

Benefits for the inclusion of Chicano studies in ethnic studies departments on the part of university administrations are obvious: it is a cost-cutting measure. Arguments for ethnic studies from Chicano/a scholars and activists are less prevalent than arguments against, although some Chicano scholars and activists believe that it is time to reconsider the relationship between Chicano studies and Latin American studies. The demographic shifts within the Latino community, for example, the number of Central American refugees, provide a compelling argument for a restructuring since there are shared concerns, including racism, poverty, educational iniquities, among Chicanos and other Latinos. Nevertheless, because the university is saving money, Mexican-American studies departments could negotiate for one or more new positions before becoming integrated into an ethnic studies department, or for a research institute or some other perquisite in exchange for saving the university money.

Affirmative action programs and the organization of Chicano studies as a field are related issues in that it is predicted that the student population will change dramatically. It was reported in the *Los Angeles Times* that "the number of underrepresented minorities enrolled at UCLA and UC Berkeley could drop 50% to 70% once the University of California's rollback of affirmative action takes effect" (Wallace 1996, A1, 18). It is predicted, in the same article, that "white" and Asian American enrollment will increase. This information was taken from two reports commissioned by the UC provost. At the time of this writing (1998), these predictions have turned out to be accurate. We must remember that affirmative action came about during the Nixon campaign and, as Aronowitz points out (1996), was cheaper than guaranteeing a decent education for all students. The demands of Chicano Studies departments include, but are not limited to, protecting affirmative action. As I write this, African-American faculty and students at Cal State San Marcos have received death threats, and racial epithets have appeared written on the walls of the campus. The campus was founded seven years ago to protect cultural diversity (*Evening News*, 11 Oct. 1996). In the Fall 1997 incoming class in the medical school at UC San Diego, there will be no African-American students.

The difficulties Chicanas and particularly Chicana lesbians have had in having their needs served by women's studies departments and Chicano studies departments point to another reason for caution in the uncritical support for the replacement of Chicano studies departments by ethnic studies. Pesquera and Segura document the ambivalence about Anglo feminism. They found that 56.4 percent of Chicanas interviewed felt that Women's Studies programs did not meet Chicanas' needs (1996, 244). Guadalupe San Miguel, in "Chicanas/os and Educational Equality," writes: "Chicana feminists on and off campus challenged sexism within the movement and within the discipline of Chicano studies an developed a more comprehensive analysis of the history and contemporary status of the Mexican-origin population (1996, 172).

In conclusion, I have argued that the real debates surrounding race, affirmative action, and the obfuscation of whiteness are about (1) responsibility for the current economic situation; and (2) the organization of knowledge, which is ultimately an issue of power. As Hardt and Negri argue in *Labor of Dionysus*, the multitude must have control over knowledge and wealth. I have argued that the discussion of reorganizing departments is not innocent or benign; it is not accidental that it occurs in the context of the dismantling of affirmative action. The extreme popularity of books such as *The Bell Curve* points to the need to look at this situation from a variety of perspectives. While the book mentions African-Americans more often, Latinos are a close, implied target. The caste system is a clear system of division, so I chose to use India as an example in a variety of ways: inner divisions had to be overcome, at least at the level of image, to solidify identity; however, this was done at great cost to women and Moslems. The question I would pose to Chicano studies departments and universities, including the department and university in and at which I teach, is, given the way in which "other" voices from within the Chicano community were downplayed or silenced in the past, even before the creation of ethnic studies, what guarantee is there that these alternative voices will be respected now, within ethnic studies? If some

Chicano/a activists fear that Chicano studies departments have become too academic and cut off from the community, how will their subsumption under the ethnic studies umbrella insure that they will strengthen links with the community? From the perspective of Chicana lesbians, are the odds better that they will be respected inside or outside of Chicano studies? Research has already shown that Chicanas do not feel well served by Women's studies departments. The larger issue for all disenfranchised groups is the obfuscation of whiteness, hiding behind the shields of "equality" and "science," and the continued unwillingness of most whites, and most white males in particular, to recognize their privilege. While the abolitionist argument may be compelling in its attention to the recognition of privilege, it is inadequate as a strategy for the inclusion of all students in a democratic, multicultural environment. A more fruitful approach is Winant's, inspired by W.E.B. Dubois, that whiteness be brought out into the open and analyzed in all its "rearticulations, representations [and] reinterpretations" (1997, 1).

Notes

1. I refer the reader to programs at San Diego State, UC San Diego, and San Francisco State. The first has separate departments in Africana studies, Native American studies and Mexican-American studies (now Chicana and Chicano studies). The other two have single ethnic studies departments.

2. Central San Diego, where my neighborhood is located, has a population of 31 percent Hispanic, 41 percent white, 15 percent black and 12 percent Asian/other. It is the most ethnically balanced area in the city. The average household income range in San Diego County is $30,339.00 to $46,778 with the highest income in white households and the lowest in black households. In the Hispanic community, 47 percent have less than a high school diploma. 1990 U.S. Census; San Diego Assoc. of Governments Demographic Characteristics Estimate. See also Braun and McKinnie (1997).

Chapter 5

Culture, Narrativity, and Assessment

What counts as culture, how a story is told, and how knowledge is assessed will be the foci of this chapter. The definition of culture will be taken from the field of anthropology, and will be shown to be broader than the definition of culture that is valorized in the classroom (Berlin 1993). As discussed in the introduction, the democratization of the art world, the de-hierachization of cultural capital, and the creation of space for popular culture and entertainment have been the "main tendencies in the institutionalization of culture" (Ahponen 1997). The complex function of culture in modern society, as both democratizing and commodified is the context for a discussion of the cultural capital that has not yet been valorized in the multicultural classroom. In order to be consider that which "counts as culture," is there a price to be paid? Will that price necessarily be commodification, just as the price of the inclusion of the non-Euroamerican child in the classroom is most often assimilation? Ahponen (1997) suggests that the deliberate crossing of boundaries could create a space for "a new kind of politics of culture." In this chapter, I will discuss this deliberate crossing of boundaries in terms of cultural capital in non middle-class, Euroamerican communities and in terms of interdisciplinary curriculum.

Many historians, anthropologists, and ethnographers are exploring a new interdisciplinary territory in which the observer situates him or herself and presents the findings in a multiplicity of voices. An example of such a work is Ruth Bejar's *Translated Woman* (1993). What these researchers are doing, in part, is to open up possibilities for how a story can be told. Derrida's *Glas* (1974) and Cortázar's *Rayuela* (1963) and *Libro de Manuel* (1973) also use experimental narrative structures and a multiplicity of voices. Such texts are much more demanding of the reader than are traditional texts. If we apply the notion of a multiplicity of voices to the classroom, knowledge itself will be redefined not as a set of facts but as the ability to "hear" a multiplicity of voices. This will imply a revalorizing of cultural capital outside of the classroom, in the community in which students live. The Argentine film *The Official Story* makes these points clearly; a traditional historian begins to question her own positionality in the classroom and later in Argentine society. By the end of the film, her quest to find the birth mother of her adopted child results in her becoming politicized about the events of the 1970s and *la guerra sucia*.

Kincheloe and Steinberg, make the important point that "the way intelligence is understood exerts a dramatic impact on schooling, teaching, and learning" (1996, 34). This insight is shared with chaos theorists, who use the example of the border of Spain and Mexico to show how one's political perspective determines measurement. Because Spain is more powerful, it is less concerned with the location of the border and the exact territory of Spain. Because Portugal is less powerful, it is more concerned with the size of its territory. The point is that, as Heisenberg already informed us, our position determines our perspective.

In the case of education, the definition of intelligence is not neutral; it is always being contested. While the definition of intelligence that serves the interest of the power structure shapes pedagogy, the curriculum, and learning, I will argue that this very definition is being challenged from below. As I argue elsewhere in this book, citizenship is being redefined to extend beyond a legal definition to a social definition; from this perspective, as Del Castillo explains, those who build community, specifically, undocumented women workers from Mexico, are providing a new way for us to understand citizenship. Similarly, the cultural capital, to use Pierre Bourdieu's term, of the oppressed is providing a new way for us to understand intelligence. In this chapter, I will argue that assessment and evaluation in education must take the "social relationship of the student to the school, the teacher, the curricula, and the tests" into account (Kincheloe and Steinberg 1996, 34). They insist that:

> [a]ny evaluation of student progress and potential must ask: how integrated is
> a child into mainstream education's discourse community? School activities,
> tasks, functions, and understandings are inseparable from wider cultural rela-
> tionships that grant them meaning (35).

I will make no attempt to give a definition of intelligence in this chapter; rather, I will refer the reader to Gardner's seven forms of intelligence (1985), Perkins' Theory of Learnable Intelligence, with its three dimensions, neural, experiential and reflective (1995), and Kincheloe and Steinberg's postformal intelligence (1996). What will be investigated is the degree to which these forms of intelligence are recognized in the educational system.

Chicana artist and former cultural commissioner of San Francisco, Amalia Mesa-Bains has discussed how the term quality, in the context of the multicultural debates, becomes a form of subterfuge that hides the desire to maintain the status quo (Hicks, 1990). I expand her discussion about the art world to a discussion of various theories accounting for school achievement. This entire discussion cannot be divorced from the social, political, and historical relationships outside of the classroom, nor can we make facile references to Greek democracy, avoiding its reliance on slaves and its exclusion of women from representation, or to U.S. democracy, which, as Cornel West (1982) reminds us, was founded on the enslavement of twenty percent of the population.

What counts as culture, how a student tells the story of what he or she knows, and how teachers evaluate the culture and stories of students all occur not in a vacuum but in the social, political, economic and historical relations between the dominant group of a society and the rest of that society. The very discussion of *achievement*, the term examined by Sonia Nieto (1996) in the phrase Stanford Achievement Test (SAT) and in educational literature in general, raises the issue of assessment. In other words, we cannot take the term "achievement" at face value, because we do not know exactly what is being measured, which makes it difficult to assess achievement. We cannot even assume that there is a real desire to find anything of value; rather, the function of the test may be to exclude and nothing else. The philosophical assumptions underlying the terms "achievement" and "assessment" are, in the first case, that one behavior constitutes an achievement and another a failure, and in the second case, that there is something of value which is to be distinguished from something which is not. My approach in this chapter will be on what is valued rather than on improved forms of standardized testing. My method in looking at what is valued will take two tacks: (1) an examination of Gardner's, Kincheloe's and Perkins's theories of intelligence in relation to assessment and (2) attention to explanations for the absence of achievement, that is, for low achievement among certain groups of students. In *Affirming Diversity*, Sonia Nieto discusses four explanatory approaches to differences in achievement: (1) deficit models (genetic and cultural); (2) social reproduction; (3) cultural compatibility and (4) resistance.

In Gardner, we find that intelligence is defined as logical-mathematical, linguistic, musical, spatial, bodily kinesthetic, interpersonal, and intrapersonal. The implications of seven forms of intelligence in the assessment of Mexican-American and Chicano students are to be made with great caution. As Nieto points out, an opening up of the definition of intelligence can benefit multicultural education and current assessment practices "that focus almost exclusively on logical-mathematical and linguistic intelligence" (1996, 140). However, she warns that we must not generalize from individual cases. If we combine this broadened definition with Bourdieu's notion of cultural capital, which will be discussed below, we will have two tools with which to better understand the value of cultural contributions from students of different backgrounds.

In Kincheloe, we find the following description of postmodern knowledge in terms of humility:

> Postmodern humility is not a passing uncertainty but a critical resistance to all presentations and interpretations that claim transhistorical certainty. In rejecting formalism's universal reason as the supreme form of cognition, critical postmodernism seeks alternative forms of thinking and knowing that are historically and socially contingent, partial as opposed to total. Postmodern teacher educators can no longer appeal to some sacrosanct body of professional knowledge that rises above all other bodies of information in value. The historically and socially specific knowledge of the practitioner must be repeated for its insight, not for its certainty (1993, 104).

Kincheloe also discusses the need in "our post-formal quest" for an overcoming of egocentrism in order to develop a connected consciousness.

According to Kincheloe, the work of Julian Jaynes can help us to understand postformal thinking. In *The Origin of Consciousness in the Breakdown of the Bicameral Mind* (1976), Jaynes lists six features of consciousness, described by Kincheloe: spatialization, such as conceptualizing time as space, excerption, or the ability to understand metonymically, the analogue "I," a constructed self which is able to function decisively in a world we also construct, the metaphor "me," our ability to conceive of ourselves in the third person, narratization, "the assignation of causes to our behavior and the granting of logical sequence to the situation we encounter, or storytelling," and conciliation, the ability to make sense of "dissimilar entities" in space.

The implications of postformal thinking in the assessment of Mexican-American and Chicano students are complex. A child raised in a strict Catholic home who has attended Catholic schools may have trouble at first with the type of uncertainty described by Kincheloe. However, writers such as Gloria Anzaldúa describe similar approaches to knowledge. Also, Native American values may overlap more with postformal than with formal thinking. Kincheloe's notion of connected consciousness is very similar to two aspects of the Mexican-American and Chicano experience. First, the Mexican family is not egocentric; the family is put before any individual member. Because this is not true in the Anglo and Euroamerican family to the same degree, Mexican-American and Chicano students have a hard time adjusting to the focus on the individual and individual achievement. If they adopt an egocentric perspective and attempt to get an education despite changes it will create with their families, such as going away to college, they will feel torn and conflicted. The Chicana movement has put great emphasis on this connectedness, which continues to be strengthened with the contributions of Chicana lesbians.

The work of Jaynes is extremely provocative in considering the consciousness of the border dweller. When the Anglo or Euroamerican thinks of the White House, as Kincheloe points out, there is a mental space created. For the border dweller with ties to Mexico, there are two spaces, the White House and Los Pinos, as well as a third form of conceptualization or multidimensional effect which is aware of both of them simultaneously. As Kincheloe writes: "Keeping in mind the social construction of consciousness, we realize that we are mentally separated from others—especially those who are culturally different—by unfamiliarity with their spatial metaphors" (1993, 133–34).

Another crucial aspect in understanding border consciousness is critical excerption. Kincheloe writes: "filters formed by the social context separate the incoming information or inventory into sections having labels" (1993, 134). He gives examples of these as sets of binary oppositions: significant/insignificant; exciting/frightening. In the border region, they function at two levels: individually, but more importantly, between the dominant culture and Mexican-American culture. An example in the border region is documented/undocumented, which has great importance to those who need to cross the border to work, and male/female, which has great importance to feminists. Although both groups could understand each other's set of oppositions, the importance given is very different. For example, a worker crossing the border without papers will be stopped whether male or female. For that reason, document/undocumented takes precedence over male/female in a major part of the everyday reality of the Mexican worker who crosses the border.

In the borderlands, the category of critical narratization is necessary for survival. Kincheloe describes it as follows:

> [I]ndividuals with a connected consciousness narratize in a way which helps us connect with individuals with backgrounds different from our own. Such a narratizing ability is based on an appreciation of the personal histories and dissimilar individual contexts of peoples from various social and cultural groups (136).

At the Barrio Logan Elementary Institute, students record oral histories of their family members. Although all of the students are first generation Mexican-Americans, their backgrounds show great diversity. The challenge for the tutors is to help the students to develop an appreciation not only of their own family histories but of students different from themselves. These difference include physical differences and class differences. One-third of the children are being raised by single mothers, including my son. Some students have many family problems, whether or not they have two parents in the home. The school at which the Institute is located is 85 percent Spanish-speaking. One-third of the families are on public assistance. The student body, however, is not homogeneous; families come from many different parts of Mexico. Students have differing abilities in the reading and writing of Spanish and English.

This category of critical conciliation is especially relevant to education in a border region. Kincheloe explains Jaynes's category as a making compatible or reconciliation of narratization (1993, 138). He refers to Jaynes's example of a mountain meadow and a tower; the two can be conciliating by having the tower rise from the meadow (1993, 136). This ability to make compatible or reconcile narratization has a similar function to what Spinoza calls the common notion. In Spinoza's "good" City, critical conciliation would be developed and practiced by citizens and would make pleasant encounters possible. In the San Diego-Tijuana border region, the bicultural student learns to reconcile narratization out of necessity. Chicano writers and artists continue to create critical conciliation in their images. Alurista and other writers who write bilingual works combine images from both sides of the border as well as referential codes, all while switching from literary to informal speech in both languages. Border writers on both sides of the border are creating a community of readers who are able to reconcile or make compatible narratization.

A fascinating category of Jaynes's is that of critical volition. Kincheloe emphasizes the understanding of the relationship of human will to the interest of power. In other words, this is not the kind of willpower to which we refer when speaking of overcoming bad habits. Rather "critical volition cultivates an awareness of the limitations on human self-direction". He argues that critical volition is achieved by those who "possess the will to act" (1993, 137). Most recently, the Chicano movement has had to fight against Propositions 209 and 187.[1]

I have used these six categories to speculate about border consciousness. If we take Jaynes seriously, simplistic views of intelligence as merely verbal or mathematical in nature must be rejected. A much more complex view of intelligence that can embrace these categories is demanded. I have shown that border dwellers are uniquely situated, by virtue of needing to develop these skills for survival in their everyday lives. For example, critical narratization can be avoided by those living in a monocultural reality. Mexican-American and Chicano students do not have this option.

In Perkins's research, we find a theory of changing or learnable intelligence. This theory discusses three dimensions of intelligence: neural, experiential, and reflective. The experiential and reflective dimensions involve change in that more experience and a greater, learned ability to be reflective increases one's intelligence. The implications of Perkins's theory of intelligence in the assessment of Mexican-American and Chicano students are great. Rather than placing Mexican-American and Chicano children into tracks for their entire time they are in school, based on test scores that supposedly predict their abilities, students will be seen as having changing intelligence. The major role of the I.Q. will change if Perkins's theory is taken seriously.

The social, political, economic, and historical relations between the dominant group of a society and the rest of that society include how the dominant group and other groups have come into contact with one another. After looking at the approaches to differences in achievement, I will address two other aspects of Nieto's analysis: (1) the distinction she makes between voluntary and involuntary immigrants and (2) what she refers to as the "Catholic School effect" (1996, 243). Voluntary immigrants (according to Ogbu, the critic from whom Nieto takes the term) come to the United States because they wish to do so, while involuntary immigrants are either brought here or forced to bend to the dictates of the U.S. government against their will (Ogbu 1986, quoted in Nieto 1996, 237). The mixture in the San Diego-Tijuana border region of recent immigrants and families that have lived in the Southwest for many generations, with many groups in between these extremes, immediately deconstructs the opposition voluntary/involuntary but makes it an important starting point for discussion. That is, it is hard to draw a line between voluntary and involuntary for those who had the border cross them, the families of Mexican descent that have been in what is now the United States for generations, and so-called voluntary immigrants who may have been driven out of Mexico for economic reasons.

The "Catholic School effect" is particularly relevant to the U.S.-Mexico border, because so many Latino parents who can afford to send their children to Catholic schools do so and because, despite some aspects of cultural incompatibility, the fact that the majority of Mexican-Americans are Catholic is a major factor in compatibility. As Nieto concludes, "What may at first glance appear to be incongruous in terms of cultural compatibility" in fact has positive results for many students in relation to non-Catholic schools (1996, 244). Nevertheless, the legacy of the Catholic Church as a colonizing tool in the region dates back to the mission system. It is a system in which Native Americans were forced into labor. Thus, while perhaps seeming to be unrelated issues, the voluntary/involuntary distinction and the educational function of the Catholic Church are deeply intertwined historically.

The preservation of the status quo through the educational system demands many tools; the most widely used tool of assessment in the schools is the standardized test. Catherine A. Lugg explains how white Protestants believed that the social hierarchy in which they were on top "selected the natural order of things" (1996, 372). She writes "The tenor of the times [late nineteenth and early twentieth century] was such that 'other' European immigrants were expected to assimilate (that is, become Anglo) as quickly as possible, and non-Whites and women were to accept their lower status" (1996, 371). She quotes two writers, Cubberly and Carl Bringham. Cubberly wrote in 1919:

These Southern and Eastern Europeans were of a very different type from the North and West Europeans who oppressed them. Largely illiterate, docile, lacking in initiative, and almost wholly without the Anglo-Saxon conceptions of righteousness, liberty, law, order, public decency and government, their coming has served to dilute tremendously our nation stock and to weaken and corrupt our political life (Cubberly 1919, 338, quoted in Lugg 1996, 373).

The new field of educational psychology and the development of standardized measures provide the setting for Bringham's contribution, the Stanford Aptitude Test. His analysis of various tests led him to the following conclusions: "Nordic groups were intellectually superior to Alpine and Mediterranean groups, Alpines were superior to Mediterraneans, and Mediterraneans were superior to Negroes" (Bringham n.p., quoted in Spring 1994, 264, quoted in Lugg 1996, 373). This hierarchy may become internalized and used by each group against the group under it; at the university where I teach, a member in the English department, it was reported to me, said that the Nobel Prize no longer meant anything since a Guatemalan woman and an African man had received it.

Standardized tests have been used to exclude the other since their inception; furthermore, there has been an ambivalence in both Spain and the United States about educating Native Americans, slaves, and workers from the time of the conquest to the present. In the mission system, Native Americans were not taught to read. Teaching a slave to read was a crime during slavery. Even though the basic literacy has been achieved by most in the twentieth century, there have still been limits placed on how far students of non-white Anglo Protestant backgrounds could continue with their educations. Lugg explains that the SAT was first used to restrict the college admission of Roman Catholic, Jewish, African-American and female students (373). In his book *Anything but Mexican*, Acuna gives an update of the standardized testing situation in relation to the Latino community in Los Angeles, part of the backdrop against which the following models will be evaluated:

[T]he white voting majority [in Los Angeles] did not want to pay for the education that restructuring the workforce would require, because that would mean educating 'the other'—in the American tradition, 'other than white.' In 1992 Latinos account for over 63 percent of the pupils in the Los Angeles Unified School District and close to 70 percent of those in elementary schools (twenty years before, only 22 percent of Los Angeles students were Latino). Many of the Latino students badly needed more educational resources. Some 200,000 of 625,000 students were Limited English Placement (LEP) students, and this number was growing by 10 percent a year. The gap in reading scores between Latino and white students in California was marked. In 1987, Latino third graders averaged scores of 500 in the California Assessment Program (CAP) math and reading tests, compared with 614 for whites. By the eighth grade the gap was 414 to 567. Latino high school seniors performed at the ninth-grade level in reading. Statewide, their high school dropout rate was double that of white students; 54 percent of the 19,381 high school students dropping out of the LAUSD in 1987/88 were Latinos. Overall, Latinos in the late 1980s had a 40 percent high school dropout rate, lower than the 46 percent among African-Americans, but much higher than the rate among Anglos. Nor were high dropout rates closely related to increased immigration of Latinos, legal or undocumented. As much as Euroangelenos wanted to scapegoat the immigrant, a 1992 report by the Department of Education, Are Hispanic Drop-out Rates Related to Migration?, found that the high Latino dropout rate would continue even if immigration slowed down (1996, 290).

In the deficit models, either the genetic background of the student is considered to be inferior, or the student's language, cultural and social class is considered to be "inadequate and negative" (Nieto 1996, 230). As Nieto points out, it is not questioned whether or not going to the library, attending museums and related activities are "in fact" enriching. She points out that the activities of children who spend summers in Jamaica or Mexico

> are not generally considered enriching, at least not for poor people. What children learn on these trips frequently is ignored by the school in spite of its potentially enriching character. The strengths that students bring to school, including knowledges of language other than English and a host of other cultural experiences and insights, are seldom considered an adequate basis for the curriculum and subsequently for their education (1996, 231). .

In relation to the Mexican-American community, this passage is very relevant. Many Latino children have families on both sides of the border and spend holidays and vacations in Mexico. The cultural knowledge that they bring back to the classroom is rich but unrecognized as cultural capital.

It is not accidental that there is an overlap between the deficit model and Bourdieu's concept of cultural capital; Bourdieu has directly addressed the work of one deficit model, that of Bernstein and his theory of restricted and expanded codes. However, unlike Bernstein, Bourdieu finds that it is the mismatch between the language of the home and the school, not the deficit of expanded codes, that can account for difficulties for working class students. James Collins explains that for Bourdieu, "language figures in education primarily as a code" (1993, 118). In Bourdieu's work with Passeron (1977), it is argued that it is the "mismatch" between the two languages, that of the home and that of school, that is an important factor in success in school (118).

> The general features of "class codes" are described by Bourdieu and Passeron in terms of "bourgeois" and "common" parlance. The former is marked by a

literary orientation, latinate vocabulary and constructions, and a striving for rare and novel expression, the latter by a situational orientation, nonlearned vocabulary, and a reliance upon shared figures of speech (Bourdieu and Passeron 1977: 116). The former, of course is much closer to the language expected in educational settings; that is, it contains much more linguistic capital in the educational field, in the educational market, where the dominant language is the official, legitimate language (Collins, 118).

Collins explains that although the bourgeois/common distinction recalls Bernstein's elaborated/restricted distinction, Bourdieu and Passeron differentiate between two types of capital. The first is linguistic capital, or "class-linked traits of speech differentially valued in a specific field or market." The second is linguistic habitus, "a class-linked relation to language" (Collins 1993, 118, 119). Ishitsuka, traces the concept of habitus to Gyorgy Lukacs's concept of class consciousness (Ishitsuka 1996, 163).[2] For Bourdieu, "the French dominant class reproduces itself through higher education" (Ishitsuka 1996, 164). Because Bourdieu emphasizes the "unification" of system and the (social) life world, Ishitsuka finds him to be in the tradition of Lukacs and Gramsci. Bourdieu exposes the dominant ideological function of modernity and modern universalism in the reproduction of French class society (Ishitsuka 1996, 164). Collins gives examples of two types of linguistic habitus: (1) that of upper-class students, including "abstraction, formalism, intellectualism, and euphemistic moderation" and 2) that of working class students, including "expressionism...mov[ing] from particular case to particular case, from illustration to parable, or shun[ning] the bombast of fine words" (118). The linguistic habitus of upper-class students serves them well in the classroom while the habitus of working-class students serves them poorly (1993, 118). Bourdieu's work is linked by Collins to the deficit model because it argues that working-class and minority children are deprived, in this case, linguistically deprived, and the source of that deprivation is in the homes and communities of these children (Collins 1993, 120). Collins's work suggests a distinction between deprivation and deficiency. It could also be argued that Bourdieu's main point is a critique of modernity, and that just because he exposes the ideological function of modernity in the reproduction of class society in France does not mean that he supports or condones it. If we see Bourdieu in the tradition of Lukacs and Gramsci, this is a reasonable viewpoint. Nevertheless, this entire discussion can form part of a critique of what in the United States is called the "linguistic deficit" hypothesis. Bourdieu's

notion of cultural capital suggests that nondominant groups can potentially increase their cultural capital not only by adopting the linguistic habitus of the upper class but also because their culture could potentially be perceived, by themselves or others, as valuable.

Ishitsuka's view that the modern situation corresponds to Protestant Europe, and that the postmodern situation corresponds to Catholic
Europe, especially the Catholic Europe of the Middle Ages, is relevant
to Latino culture in the border region in that Latino culture is predominantly Catholic. Ishitsuka extends his argument to include a link
between the Protestant "form of intellectualism" and the identity principle, and the Catholic "form of intellectualism" and nonidentity or
the postmodern principle of difference (1996, 172). Many border artists have noted and found as a source of inspiration the postmodern
elements in border culture. In relation to the situation of the Chicano
student, the issue of social class and a class-linked relation to language
is very important. Chicano students are most often first-generation
college students and working class. Pride in the cultural capital of the
Chicano community has been central in the Chicano movement.

Nieto argues that the deficit approach needs to be supplemented by
the work of Bourdieu and his definitions of the three forms of cultural
capital: (1) "dispositions of the mind and body; (2) "cultural goods,
such as pictures, books, and other material objects"; and (3) "educational qualifications" (1996, 233). In the San Diego-Tijuana border
region, there is a paucity of educational qualifications in terms of college degrees in the Latino community, but there is a rich inheritance
of cultural goods such as art, music, and public murals.

This brings us to the social reproduction model. Nieto refers to
research during the 1970s by such scholars as Bowles, Gintis, and
Spring. The basic premise of the theory that informs this model is
that the role of schools is to keep the poor in their place and to teach
them to become good workers. The children of the dominant classes
are taught the skills of management in preparation for their futures as
managers of the working class: "Schools therefore reproduce the status quo and not only reflected structural inequalities based on class,
race, and gender, but also actually maintained them (Nieto 1996, 233).
In relation to the Mexican-American community, this view is shared
by many Chicano/as. One way in which the status quo is preserved is
in the teaching of languages. Spanish is considered a positive attribute
for the English-speaking student, who may one day be in positions of
management of Spanish-speaking workforces.

Nieto admits that the reproduction model is a compelling model, but objects to it to the degree that it "assumes that schooling is simply imposed from above and accepted from below" (1996, 234). In San Diego, the situation of the imposition of schooling is more complex, as evidenced by the teacher's strike of 1996 and the continuing attempts of parents to fight for better schools. At the university level, as well, there have been attempts at resistance, such as the occupation for over a year by students of part of the campus after 189 tenured faculty were fired by President Day at San Diego State University in 1993. Teaching assistants at both UC San Diego and San Diego State have tried to form unions and have fought for better conditions and health care.

Most interesting from a border perspective is Nieto's conclusion that theories of social and cultural reproduction do not take community struggles into account, such as the fights for integrated schools, bilingual education, multicultural education and access to education for females (1996, 235). To this list we could add recruitment of Latinos and other non-Anglo students from high schools into the university and the building and maintenance of cultural capital by community-based organizations such as the Centro Cultural de la Raza, the Chicano Federation Community Clinic, the Sherman Heights Community Center, the Barrio Logan Elementary Institute, and the César Chávez School, to name just a few. Chicano Park is another example of a community struggle that is linked to cultural capital, particularly because it is the site of so many murals. Chicano artists gained national and international prominence in the 1980s through the work of the Border Art Workshop/*Taller de arte fronterizo*. Chicano writers from San Diego, Los Angeles, San Francisco and other cities have also received international attention, especially in Europe. Acuna (1996) lists many such examples of Chicano cultural capital including the efforts of Chicanos to preserve the Siquieros mural *America Tropical*.

In the cultural compatibility model, it is argued that there is an antagonistic relationship or clash between home and school culture (Nieto 1996, 235). According to this logic, the more similar or compatible the two cultures, the more successful the student will be; conversely, the more that the "experiences, skills, and values" of the student differ from those of school, the less successful the student will be (235). Nieto finds the cultural compatibility model to be more optimistic than the deficit theory of genetic inferiority or the economic reproduction theory, both of which are deterministic.

In relation to the Mexican-American community, creating cultural compatibility between the home and the classroom might mean cooperative learning, attention to the importance of the Mexican family, attention to Mexican culture and history, and to Chicano politics. At the Barrio Logan Elementary Institute and at Perkins Elementary in Barrio Logan, this compatibility has been nurtured. At Perkins in 1997, Martin Luther King Day was celebrated with the Mexican Hat Dance and a funk piece played by the vice-principal and his Afro-Cuban Salsa All-Stars band. A Latino/African-American Boy's Club has been formed; any student is welcome to attend meetings.

As Nieto points out, the Mexican-American community is not homogeneous; there are differences between Mexican-Americans (1996, 14). The creation of cultural compatibility between the classroom and the home is a difficult goal because there are differences in homes within the communities of, for example, the ninety-five languages spoken by students in Los Angeles. At the level of high school, there are gender differences as well. Although Nieto does not address this issue, the needs of gay and lesbian Latinos in the classroom are different from those of heterosexual students. Could cultural compatibility embrace Chicana lesbian culture through the teaching, for example, of Anzaldúa's work?

In the resistance model, first described by Paul Willis in *Learning to Labor* (1981), the refusal to learn may be seen as an act of political resistance. From this perspective, negative attitudes towards school that are entrenched over time must be seen in light of the relationship between the dominated group and the dominant group. Willis studied working-class boys in England. Nieto lists misbehavior, vandalism, and poor relationship with teachers as examples of resistance (1995, 240). Collins discusses Willis's work in the following terms:

> The cultural and discursive forms through which tough, working class males subvert pedagogic authority are educationally disabling, hence reproductive, since they limit the young men to the industrial labor of their fathers. Yet, through these forms the young men also simultaneously achieve a penetration of educational ideology, a real, practical critique of the false promises of educational meritocracy. Hence there is a contradiction: the students are simultaneously (self-)disabled and achieve collective insight, in advance of their conforming peers or the liberal staff who would "reach them" (1993, 127).

In relation to the Mexican-American community, the resistance to education remains very strong, and crosses over into what Ogbu refers to as "the burden of acting White" (quoted in Nieto 1996, 29).

writes: "There is little benefit, in terms of peer relationships, in being successful students" (239). It often divides recent Mexican immigrants from Mexican-American and Chicano students. Although this difference is not addressed directly by Nieto in her discussion of the immigrant vs. the "minority" experience, a distinction which will be discussed in greater detail later in this chapter, it is significant in the Latino community. The recent immigrant has more in common with voluntary immigrants, while Mexican-American and Chicano students have more in common with involuntary immigrants. Even parents may be divided along these lines. Active parents may be ridiculed for participating in school activities by other parents. At a meeting of the Barrio Logan Education Institute, an active parent reported that other mothers referred to parents who went to meetings at Perkins Elementary School as "women who had nothing else to do with their lives."[3] Mexican-American and Chicano students are called *pochos* in Mexico. This is a derogatory term that encompasses inferior linguistic abilities with regard to speaking Spanish, a dilution of the culture and the stigma of living with the enemy, the United States. Although all ethnic minorities experience some discomfort upon returning to the country of their origin, because Mexico shares a 2,000-mile border with the United States, there is much more contact and much more opportunity for humiliation of this kind. There is a very high drop-out rate in the Latino communities of Los Angeles and San Diego. As Nieto writes, "the most extreme form of refusing education is dropping out" (1996, 240).

In relation to the U.S.-Mexico border region, research about "the Catholic School effect" is significant because so many Latinos, if they are able to afford it, send their children to Catholic schools. Nieto explains that in certain aspects, a Catholic school is culturally incompatible for a Latino student: "Bilingual programs are often unavailable; the classes are generally overcrowded; and formal environments that stress individual excellence over cooperation are usually the order of the day" (1996, 244). She refers to several studies showing that even poor Latinos achieve more in Catholic schools, when achievement is measured by higher SAT scores, rates of graduation, and scores above the national mean. She concludes that Catholic schools "tend to offer all students a less differentiated curriculum, less tracking, and more academic classes" (1996, 244).

Finally, I want to address the distinction Nieto makes between voluntary and involuntary immigrants. She refers to Ogbu's definition, that voluntary immigrants may include all European and some southeast Asian, African and Central American immigrants. He contrasts these with "those who have been conquered or colonized," including "American Indians, Africans, Mexicans, and Puerto Ricans" (Ogbu 1986, quoted in Nieto 1996, 237). In the U.S.-Mexico border region, this distinction is complicated by many factors, including: (1) the Southwest used to be part of Mexico; (2) during the Great Depression, Mexicans were among those immigrants who suffered forced repatriation. Acuna explains that Mexican migrants around 1900 "were simultaneously pushed by economic conditions in their own countries and pulled by the availability of jobs in the United States" (Acuna 1996, 109).

I have discussed how what counts as culture, how a student tells the story of what he or she knows, and how teachers evaluate the culture and stories of students all occur in the social, political, economic and historical relations between the dominant group of a society and the rest of that society. The function of the test appears to be to exclude. I have referred the reader to Gardner's seven forms of intelligence, Perkins's Theory of Learnable Intelligence, with its three dimensions, neural, experiential and reflective, and Kincheloe and Steinberg's postformal intelligence. What was investigated was how these forms were or more often were not recognized in the educational system. While Gardner's seven forms of intelligence may function as a way to broaden the definition of intelligence, and eventually, assessment, Nieto is convincing when she warns us not to generalize quickly about different types of intelligence and students of certain cultural groups. Rather, we must recognize the differences between students in the same cultural groups. Perkins's Theory of Learnable Intelligence could possibly help Mexican-American and Chicano students, as well as all other students who are categorized as non gifted, slow learners and other terms which imply an unchangeable identity. Most promising for preparing not just Mexican-American and Chicano children but all children for the multicultural, postmodern future is the work of Kincheloe and Steinberg on postformal intelligence. Drawing on Jaynes' discussion of human consciousness, Kincheloe extrapolates pedagogical implications from what he calls postformal intelligence. Postformal intelligence is not based on certainty. Like Adorno's theory of nonidentity, it can function to reveal what the power structure attempts to conceal. Adorno and Ishitsuka, in his discussion of Bourdieu, stress the importance of nonidentity in their critiques of modernism.

Postformal pedagogy recognizes the "double consciousness" of the oppressed. In relation to the border, I have referred to this double consciousness as a multidimensional perspective. The "double consciousness" of the oppressed is an important part of the cultural capital of Mexican-Americans and Chicanos/as.

Most important for our discussion of intelligence and assessment is Kincheloe's view that "[t]he concepts of subjugated knowledge or difference form a starting point for a postmodern commitment to intelligence, to rewriting the traditional notions of cognition" (1993, 74). His reference to the work of Maria Mies (1986) reminds us that using the voices of the subjugated can "empower those who are presently powerless and . . . validate oppressed ways of thinking that open new cognitive doors to everyone" (Kincheloe 1993, 73).

Having considered the four approaches to differences in achievement, the deficit models (genetic and cultural), the social reproduction model, the cultural compatibility model, and the resistance model, along with the "Catholic School effect," and the distinction between voluntary and involuntary immigrants, it has become clear that, as Nieto writes "It is necessary to understand school achievement as contextual and as an interactive, personal, cultural, political, and societal process in which all of these factors affect one another in sometimes competing and contradictory ways" (1996, 246). If we consider the voluntary/involuntary dichotomy and the Nordic/other dichotomy, voluntary Nordic would be the most privileged with regard to success in school and involuntary/other would be the least. Considering these two dichotomies together is helpful in understanding how Punjabis (voluntary/other), could still succeed, and why involuntary/other would have much greater difficulty. This could also partially account for the differences between recently arrived immigrants from Mexico (voluntary/other) and Chicanos/as (involuntary/other). To put it more clearly, we cannot simply compare achievement in school of Mexican-American students, who must contend with the very complex political, historical and economic relationship the United States has with Mexico, with Punjabi students, who have a very complex relationship to Indian culture but a relatively less complex one with the United States. If we expand our notion of intelligence to postformal intelligence, and our assessment of intelligence to include Gardner's seven forms of intelligence and Bourdieu's notion of cultural capital, then we will broaden our ability to understand the needs, abilities, and potential of not just Mexican-American, Chicano/a, and Punjabi students, but all students.

In the San Diego-Tijuana border region, many approaches to education result in the success of Mexican-American students in a traditional sense, including the decision of parents to send their children to magnet schools (including participation in GATE) to schools in Tijuana, to Catholic schools, and to private schools. However, the majority of Mexican-American students are funneled into environments in which they do not succeed. The cultural compatibility model suggests many multicultural classroom activities and lesson plans, but without understanding the classroom in its relation to the society outside of the classroom, as the social reproduction model does. One fruitful way in which these two can mutually inform each other is by using the concept of cultural capital from the social reproduction model and including that cultural capital in the classroom as part of the cultural compatibility model. The Mexican-American community, stigmatized by the deprivation model due to poverty, and objectively in a subordinate position to Euroamerican culture, can be better understood by referring to these models. The deficit model is important as a model to reject. Many children in the San Diego-Tijuana border region have family on both sides of the border and spend holidays and vacations in Mexico. All of this should be valued as cultural capital and should play a role. Despite the critiques of the social reproduction model, it is a very useful model for describing conditions in this region. Furthermore, it is a perspective that many Latino/a parents share. The "Catholic School effect" should become a challenge to all progressive, public school educators. Unless a poor Latino child can be guaranteed a good education in a public school, it is unreasonable to ask parents to send their children to public schools. However, the need for students to be computer literate may put those in private and Catholic schools at a disadvantage, because only public magnet schools can afford state-of-the-art computer labs.

I want to conclude with the arguments of Freire (1992) and Kincheloe. Our assessment of educational institutions should not conceived of in terms of individual students, but in the ability of classes and schools to educate all students. The consciousness that will make this possible, a critical postmodern consciousness, is a connected consciousness. It is based on an ethics of solidarity that creates networks and alliances. This ability to make compatible or reconcile narratization has a similar function to what Spinoza calls the common notion. We can find leaders in the development of this consciousness in oppressed voices, in those with "double consciousness," and in those who are situated on geographic, cultural and linguistic borders. In Spinoza's "good" City, critical conciliation would be developed and practiced by citizens and would make pleasant encounters possible.

Notes

1. Proposition 209 dealt with affirmative action; Proposition 187 dealt with the social services available for undocumented workers.

2. Shoji Ishitsuka (1996) discusses Bourdieu's work in relation to the work of Niklaus Luhmann, Jürgen Habermas, and Anthony Giddens.

3. Barrio Logan Elementary Institute Parent Meeting, Perkins Elementary, San Diego, 22 March 1997. As a parent in the group, I witnessed tremendous dedication on the part of some of the parents, including a father who donated ice from the company where he worked for snow cones. Not only did he support her education, but he was illiterate, and she, a third grader, was teaching him to read.

Chapter 6

Immigration, Emigration and Literary Analysis: Voices of the Not-Quite-White

In this chapter, I will remind the reader of West's view (1982) that we are living at the end of the Age of Europe which began with the expulsion of the Jew. Does this mean that we are living at the end of the Age of White Hegemony? Braidotti (1995) extends West's discussion of the process of "the decentering of Europe" with her own conclusion: "The world will never be white again, nor will it be masculine or Euro-centric again" (4). As Vron Ware writes (1977) "ideas about whiteness and the various constructions of white identity can offer new avenues of thought and action to those working to understand and dismantle systems of racial domination." Nevertheless, even to begin this endeavor is fraught with peril. Aldon Lynn Nielson points out the dilemma. On the one hand, "the constitution of the white subject is to a great extent a literary project" (1988, 10). Yet, on the other hand, even as he concludes his analysis of this project, he writes that to address the construction of whiteness means working within "the initial dialectic that discourse sets up" and giving it primacy, "if only in the hope that someone might strike it down" (164). He refers to the work of both Hans Gadamer and Jean-Francois Lyotard as he describes the linguistic prison in which we find ourselves as we face the problems of the language of description (164). Gadamer (1982) has written about the extent to which language preforms thought and Lyotard (1971) has addressed the impossibility of reforming language since we must use the tool of language to transform it. Nielson's conclusion will be our starting point, that "we should become W.E.B. Dubois's double conscious dreamer, able to view both sides of the veil of language at once" (Nielson 1988, 164). Not only is whiteness linked to literature, but it is also linked to the formation of working-class identity, as will be discussed below. A social hierarchy based on race and class distinctions mitigates against the development of double consciousness, but that is what gives a unique perspective to the border dweller and the subject with multiple cultural and ethnic identities. The confusion about what whiteness means, the definition of a legal worker and a legal resident, the ambivalence of the state about which part of the population to educate, and the inability to decide whether or not to educate workers—that is, if educated workers make more productive workers—are all symptomatic of the inadequacy of the melting-pot metaphor of culture of the United States.

Although I am taking the term "not quite white" from Elsie Michie's (1996) discussion of identity in *Jane Eyre*, I am extending it to biracial and mulatto subjects. Michie in turn had borrowed the "not quite/not white" concept from Homi Bhabha [1984]. I would go so far as to extend it to those writers who have, even at the risk of "presum[ing] too much," to use Nielson's term, attempted to link their situations to those of the nonwhite. According to Ronald Walters, "Whites are . . . individuals whose individualism is enhanced in relationship to non-Whites because it is linked to the matrix that includes wealth, access to resources, and control over the dominant institutions of society" (1996, 3). Using this definition, we can see that a gay man in the 1950s certainly did not have control over the dominant institutions of society; following this logic, a writer such as John Weiners, who, according to Nielson (1988, 157), accepted "many of the white assertions about blackness as being adequate referential descriptions and then want[ed] those same descriptions applied to themselves," plays a significant role in undermining the boundaries of whiteness. Weiners writes "We may sing our songs/of love like the black mama/on the juke box, after all/what have we got left" (1972, quoted in Nielson 1988, 157). I find Weiners's dilemma to be a self-fashioning version of the problem of the language of description. Nielson finds Adrienne Rich, especially in her early work, to have presumed too much in her identification of her black nurse as her black mother. I agree with Nielson, and yet I find these crossover attempts, however awkward, to be examples of border subjectivities and a refusal of the black/white dichotomy. Walters explains that individual skills and other factors determine how successful the use of these advantages is, but nevertheless, the degree to which they exist for whites is much greater than for blacks and non-Whites (3). He explains that "White" people were created in America out of many ethnic groups: Irish, German, Slav, French, Spanish, Nordic (1). In his review of David R. Roediger's *The Wages of Whiteness: Race and the Making of the American Working Class*, Daniel J. Walkowitz refers to Roediger's argument that there is a parallel development of American working-class identity and the sense of whiteness. He explains that, following Herbert Gutman and George Rawick, Roediger views whiteness as a trade-off for the alienation and exploitation workers have been forced to endure. In other words, the status, or skin-privilege, associated with light skin became a supplementary psychological wage within a system of class relationships (Walkowitz 1994, 98).

Border regions are excellent sites for the study of relationships between class, race and the law. Many have commented on the way in which racism is being replaced by anti-immigrant sentiments. Catherine Orenstein draws a parallel between Mexicans in California and Haitians in the Dominican Republic. The denial of welfare and education to suspected undocumented workers, Proposition 187, according to Orenstein, is symptomatic of tension at the border (1995, 601). On a global level, as Adelaida Del Castillo has argued, immigration, women and the postnational era are all linked. Leobardo Saravia Quiroz (1990) argues in his essay on the border police novel that the border region ignores the morality of the drug situation in terms of good or bad and merely accepts it as a given, which subverts a moralistic Western perspective. Similarly, following Del Castillo, the ignoring of immigration laws by immigrant women from Mexico must be seen as a reality, beyond good and evil.

Orenstein focuses on race in her discussion of Haitians in the Dominican Republic. She explains that, historically, Dominicans have taken pride in their European heritage, and reminds us that C.L.R. James explained some of the 128 divisions of the offspring of white and black in his book *The Black Jacobins*. Orenstein observes that like Mexicans in the U.S. border region, Haitians in the Dominican Republic are both recruited and rejected (1995, 7).

In a Foucauldian sense, the border, the most strategic and contested site of immigration, is also the site which produces identity for not just undocumented immigrants, but serves to discipline and punish documented immigrants as well. The border symbolically creates an identity in the context of the following oppositions: outsider/insider, illegal/legal, citizen/noncitizen—and most insidious, status/nonstatus. The purview of the latter category, in which the designation of no status at all may be conferred, can extend beyond the borders of the United States—Theoretically, a child could have no status in the U.S. or the country of origin of the parents. Furthermore, the limits put on immigrants in terms of employment, housing, education, and citizenship are only slightly different from those put on "legal" Chicano/ as and other citizens.

As border writing, border art, and Chicana poetry and prose all exemplify, there are limits of employment, housing and education in the Chicano/a community. To put this in the context of the university, 4/10 percent, that is 255 out of the 57,000 tenured faculty in the United States, are Chicanas (1996, Pesquera and Segura 243). Tey Diana Rebolledo points out that as of 1995, the *PMLA* has not published a single article on a Chicana, nor has *Critical Inquiry*. She estimates that there are about twenty Chicana literary critics in the United States (1995, 1).

The responses of writers to the immigration experience are varied and include the assimilated converso, the naturalized citizen who lives in a Latino neighborhood and the binational dweller who does not give up a close relationship to Mexico. Nevertheless, the person of Mexican descent living in the United States is often the target of racism from Anglos, for whom his citizenship is always in question, and contempt from Mexicans, for whom he/she is a pocho (Americanized person of Mexican descent who is perceived as having lost the language of Spanish and the culture of Mexico). The liminal subject has been the object of derision and suspicion. Kathleen Pfeiffer rejects the dichotomy of blackness as an authentic identity and whiteness as an opportunistic one. In her study of the 1912 novel by James Weldon Johnson, *Autobiography of an Ex-Colored Man* she uses the ambivalence of the ex-colored man about both whiteness and blackness as a way to understand the nuances of the novel, particularly that "[h]is assertive self-determination taps into a strand of American ideology which heretofore has been unavailable to blacks" (Pfeiffer 1996, 2). What makes Johnson's text even more complex is that it was first published anonymously and assumed to be an autobiography by its early readers; yet, in fact, it is "[n]ot strictly fiction[al]," nor is it "entirely autobiographical" (1).

The ambivalence that Pfeiffer finds so rich in helping us to understand "the intersection of race, individualism, and national identity," and the way in which the protagonist's racial vacillation is "both sympathetic to many races and independent of any single racial affiliation" is interesting when read against texts analyzed by Ware. Ware looks at two texts commenting on the murder of an English woman on an African game reserve, including one written by her father, and a book by a journalist about the situation of two English citizens taken by their Yemeni father to Yemen to be married. Ware writes: "English feminists writing about the position of Hindu and Muslim women in India revealed ways in which they positioned themselves in relation to nonwhite, non-Christian femininity, and also how they contributed to enduring constrictions of Asian femininity as passive, mute, submissive, and wronged. In doing so they also defined their own femininity that derived form their position as English women, Christians, wives, and daughters" (1997, 8). Just as colonial rule brought English, Christian, white women together with Hindu and Moslem women in India, so the U.S.-Mexico border brings together Anglo and Latino women.

In her paper "The Proof of Whiteness: More Than Skin Color," Roxanne Dunbar-Ortiz traces the origins of white supremacy to *la limpieza de la sangre* (purity or cleanliness of blood) and the significance of that concept in the Christian Crusades against Islam/Africa. Dunbar-Ortiz recounts the United States origin story as beginning with the Calvinist Protestants, specifically the Ulster-Scott Calvinist settler/colonizers of Northern Ireland and the western lands of the British North American colonies, "doing God's will and forging into the promised land, killing the heathen (first the Irish, then the Native Americans)." She concludes that "[t]o the extent that African-Americans and immigrants are allowed (and willing) to embrace and embody U.S. patriotism [defined as linked to white supremacy] they may be accepted as conversos, as the Spanish Inquisition termed those who had forsaken their "filthiness" for "cleanliness of blood" (Dunbar-Ortiz 1996, n.p.). As a fourth generation Sicilian, I find this argument compelling because it accounts very well for the racism in Italy towards southern Italians and especially Sicilians. The end of Arab rule in Sicily was accompanied by the expulsion of the Moors and the Jews. Nevertheless, many Jews stayed and lived as *conversos*. There are still Sicilian surnames linked to families of Arabic and Jewish origin, such as Farrugg and D'Angelo. That is, these families took on Sicilian names. Dunbar-Ortiz links her analysis of white supremacy to colonialism, which certainly seems relevant to the case of colonialism in Mexico and Latin America in general.

While whiteness is now beginning to be studied, Sylvia Wynter pointed out nearly twenty years ago that "whiteness is taken as a given, rather than as a striking phenomenon calling for extensive research." Wynter describes the double bind in which the white master and the poor white each found themselves in the context of slavery in the United States:

> On the one hand, the sacred injunction of the Constitution declaimed that all men were created equal. On the other hand, the more and everyday conventions, ethics, values constituted him as a man, only as white and therefore only on condition that he distanced himself as far as possible from the symbolic negation of manhood and whiteness—the black (Wynter 1979, 150).

Wynter argues that the way the contradiction was resolved in "the settler" who was also "the bearer of the egalitarian creed" was the projection of the Sambo/Nat stereotype: "By constructing Sambo as the negation of responsibility, the slave master legitimated his own role as the responsible agent acting on behalf of the irresponsible minstrel." The image of rebellion, found in the stereotype of Nat Turner, "legitimated the use of force as a necessary mechanism for ensuring regular steady labor" (1979, 151). In the border region, the stereotypes of the "lazy Mexican" and the violent gang member function in a similar manner. This contradiction is that same one that plagues the neoconservative, as Winant explains in his essay "Beyond Blue Eyes" (1997). Another example of the legitimation of the use of violence in relation to stereotyping can be found in Ware's discussion of the writer and activist Ida B. Wells. According to Wells's analysis of lynching, lynching was a form of repression that drew strength from an implied justification: The hanging of black men was legitimized by stories of rape and assault of white women by black men (Ware 1997, 9).

Wynter also explains how literacy is a crucial aspect in maintaining "the norm of master, of which the white skin is merely a sign" (1979, 152): "The plantation order which made it illegal for a slave to learn to read and become educated, which exhausted the black with relentless work, then produced empirical evidence of the Negro's "lack of intellectual faculties" (152). Wynter distinguishes her view from Aronowitz's and Baudrillard's, both of whom have argued that "the industrial workplace is the very site of the ideological domination of the worker" (1979, 156). Wynter finds the source and origin of the ideological domination of the worker to be in the plantation model. I find that in the U.S.-Mexico border, the industrial workplace and the plantation-model merge.

The understanding of the semiotic nature of white skin, that it is a sign for maintaining power, can explain the very contradictory views about race that often distinguish statements made by whites and non whites. A workshop director on race relations, Charley Flint, who identifies herself as "a black, feminist sociologist from a Southern working class background," makes the following statement about the different ways white people name themselves: "Jewish, Italian, Irish, women, hey, working class, as anything, it seems, but white" (1996, n.p.). Whether or not she would agree with the analyses of many critics about the shifting nature of the term white is less important than the way in which her statement registers how white skin functions in a semiotic system of visual signifiers. The white person who does not want to be labeled white, she speculates, fears that being white is equivalent with being a racist, and therefore wants to get away from the label (1).

Not only does the border provide the source of ideological domination of the worker, by creating the possibility of a job, the fear of being deported, and the fear of fighting for rights but it creates the identity of the border crosser/dweller. In the current political climate, a child of Mexican descent currently living in the United States could have no status in the United States or the country of origin of the parents. This nonstatus position is the position of absolute lack described by Wynter:

> The terror of lack, a terror ceaselessly produced by the social and cultural machine of the system, is put into play. Sambo is produced as the symbol of the Negative Other, the very principle of lack. One must strive to attain to the pure white as Full Being, without any security that this cannot be lost, that one cannot fall off into the dark (1979, 153).

She quotes Deleuze and Guattari:

> Lack (manque) is created, planned and organized in and through social production . . . it is never primary; production is never organized on the basis of a preexisting need or lack . . . The deliberate creation of lack as a function of the market economy is the art of the dominant class" (153, quoted in Wynter n.d., n.p.).

It is in the voices of the "not quite white," the immigrant whose identity is still constantly called into question, and the border dweller in whom we hear the resonances of the way in which whiteness, the literary text, and social class overlap. As Gary Soto writes in his poem "Mexican Begin Jogging" 1996), when he worked in a factory, whenever the INS would show up, his boss would tell him "OK, it's time for you to go over the fence," even though he was a citizen. While the U.S. citizen of Irish, German, Slav, French, Spanish and Nordic descent no longer suffers such experiences, the fact the each of these groups were once immigrants, outsiders, and not English attests to the malleability of the category of "white."

This brings us back to the concerns listed at the beginning of the chapter: (1) the confusion about what whiteness means; (2) the definitions of a legal worker and a legal resident, and (3) the ambivalence of the state about which part of the population to educate. We have seen that the construction of whiteness can be approached in relation to literary texts and the formation of working-class identity. As noted earlier, the corporate state seems unable to decide whether or not to educate workers, that is, if educated workers make more productive workers. The state is also ambivalent about the legality of immigrant workers and both invites and rejects them. These fractures in the state are registered most poignantly in the literary works of the "not quite white."

Chapter 7

Pedagogical Implications of the Deleuzo-Guattarian Perspective: From Negri to Darder

I cannot put forward a totalizing theory that would pretend to resolve all of the disparities that have arisen in the previous chapters, nor do I wish to do so. Nevertheless, I want to point out what is valuable and what is still lacking, perhaps, in the work of critics already considered and in the recent work being done in the area of citizenship in multicultural societies and in a world in which the nation as a concept is becoming outmoded. According to Rosi Braidotti (1995, 4), "The interesting thing about the process of the trans-national economy is it has accelerated the decline of the nation state and it has laid the foundations for a different form of international order." I will look at different theories of the state and its relationship to education and to labor. As Hardt and Negri write in *Labor of Dionysus*, in relation to feminist critiques of marxism, "the very concept of labor is mobile and historically defined through contestation. In this sense the labor theory of value is equally a value theory of labor" (9). I will discuss these issues in relation to the U.S.-Mexico border and I will use the definition of Elizabeth Martínez and Ed McCaughan (1990) of the Mexican-American and Chicano working class as the most stable element of the transnational working class.

Before beginning the analysis of various theories of the state and citizenship and a discussion of critical pedagogy, I want to address briefly the role of the state in relation to education, law, and labor, and to put forward an expanded definition of labor. The context of this discussion is the postmodern state. In the state, the educational and the juridical overlap. The link I want to make between schools and the courts is made by Gutiérrez-Jones in *Rethinking the Borderlands* (1995). He refers to the work of John Guillory (1987, quoted on 11), who argues that both the schools and the courts "maintain social inequalities"; the way they do this is not by reproducing social relations but the institution itself. Gutiérrez-Jones continues: "While both the school and the court produce a means of accessing the traditions of culture and law, these institutions perpetuate specific relations to both which differ for different people" (11). Both Gutiérrez-Jones (1995) and Catherine MacKinnon (1989) address the issue of how Chicanos and women, respectively, know through their experience that they will be treated differently; "they both support civil rights activism and express fear about legal institutions (1995, 11). In an essay written in 1975, Negri argues against the double nature of the State, "'good' when it assists us and 'bad' when it finances private capitalists" (182). At the time of this writing, he argues that the State is "the organic structure of the power of the ruling class" (183). MacKinnon will criticize this view. For Gutiérrez-Jones, it is by studying legal rhetoric that we can engage in cultural critique: "A battle is taking place in which rhetorical options severely limit the conception and institution of reform . . ." (1995, 12). The response of proponents of multicultural education to the function of the schools as maintaining social inequalities is critical pedagogy.

It is my intention to lay the groundwork for a richer understanding of labor, to which Hardt adds the concept of "affective labor." Hardt and Negri discuss the notion of "affective labor" with reference to "new qualities of laboring processes" and "new instances of immaterial labor" and note that "we can begin to recognize the alternative circuits of social valorization and the new subjectivities that arise from these processes" (1994, 12). They give two examples of a new kind of use value, female workers in hospitals and AIDS activists. The example of the nurse, whose relationship to the patient is characterized by intense emotion as well as highly skilled knowledge of technology, calls for a new understanding of work and subjectivity. Hardt and Negri direct us towards Donna Haraway's cyborg, which she describes in her well-known essay "A Cyborg Manifesto." It is here that we remember that "labor is both subjection and subjectivation" (Hardt and Negri 1994, 12). In the case of the AIDS activist, Hardt and Negri point out that many have become "expert in scientific and medical issues and procedures" related to AIDS (1994, 13). In both cases, the nurse and the activist, there is a high level of technico-scientific labor, to use their term, that demands reconceptualizing subjectivity. In this context, the subject has both the affective ability to nurture and heal and the scientific and technology ability to support this work.

I want to extend Hardt and Negri's argument to speculation about the cyborg teacher of the next century in the multicultural classroom and the *maquila* (from *maquiladora*, or factory built on the Mexican side of border, foreign-owned) worker. The class of the cyborg teacher is taught partly in person and partly on video and through the Internet. Information, including syllabi and course work can be accessed in many languages. Assessment already takes place through e-mail student journals. This teacher may resemble the nurse in terms of her highly skilled knowledge of technology; she or he may have a relationship with students characterized by intense emotion. Hardt and Negri write: "The cyborg is now the only model available for theorizing subjectivity" (14). The term "cyborg" captures what Hardt and Negri refer to as cybernetic appendages [that] are incorporated into the technologized body, becoming part of its nature" (10). The teacher of the future in the multicultural classroom, who will use electronic journals, distance learning and other forms of media as part of teaching, will be "both human and machine" (14).

By turning to the notion of the cyborg, Hardt and Negri leave an opening for discussing many deterritorialized, transnational women workers, including Southeast Asian factory workers and Mexican women who work in the *maquilas*. Theorizing about a new kind of use value and a new form of subjectivity should include these workers as well. In my essay "Robo-raza at the Crossroads" (1992), I suggest that this border cyborg should be the model of the worker, not Marx's male factory worker. Through robo-raza, racism as an issue can be addressed along with an affective theory of labor.

My thesis is that there is an analogous new kind of use value in the Mexican transnational and *maquila* workers and that it is also technico-scientific and nurturing; this new kind of use value is the community-building that is creating communities that do not respect national boundaries. Just as Hardt and Negri's example are gender specific, in that the example of the nurses refers to women, and the example of AIDS activists refers mostly to gay men, these community builders are women. Whether these women actually live on the border or are deterritorialized and live between two cultures regardless of geographic location, they have access to a border sensibility. Theoretically, these women and cyborg teachers could create learning communities inside and outside of educational institutions.

My method in this chapter will be to look at: (1) theories of the state, including critiques of law and the state; (2) new definitions of citizenship; and (3) critical pedagogy. By critical pedagogy, I am referring specifically to that strategy that is being put forward by radical pedagogues as a way to analyze rhetoric, including legal rhetoric, and to engage in cultural critique; related to critical pedagogy in the field of literature are debates about the canon. I want to consider these three areas of inquiry in relation to each other and specifically in relation to border regions. I will focus on three studies of the state, one that is informed by a feminist perspective, one that studies the state in relation to the nation in multiethnic societies and one that is put forward by Hardt and Negri. I will use three recent studies of citizenship by Meehan, Kymlicka, and Spinner as focal points in a discussion of citizenship. The final section of this chapter will be on critical pedagogy. I will look at an essay by Jameson on the literary canon and the work of Darder and her use of the term "critical thinking." I will also look at *Rethinking the Borderlands*. Although it does not purport to be a Chicano theory of the state, it is an analysis of the criminalization of the Chicano, and when read in relation to MacKinnon, is very suggestive of what a Chicano/a theory or border theory of the state might be.

The first theory of the state, MacKinnon's seeks to formulate a feminist theory of the state. Noting that "feminism has no theory of the state" she goes on to say that even though Marxism has a theory of value, it has "a problematic theory of the state" (1989, 157). On this last point, she is closer to the view of Norberto Bobbio, who, according to Negri, finds no Marxist theory of the State than to Negri, who finds in Marx "the basis of a very radical critique of law and the State" (1994, 4). According to MacKinnon "until recently, most marxist theory has tended to consider as political that which occurs between classes and the state as the instrument of the economically dominant class." She maintains that for Marxists now, the state is "relatively autonomous" (1989, 158). MacKinnon writes "feminism has not confronted, on its own terms, the relation between the state and society within a theory of social determination specific to sex" (1989, 159).

Similarly, the Chicano movement has not confronted on its own terms the relation between the state and society within a theory of social determination specific to race—in this case, Chicano identity. In postperestroika Europe, a border theory of the state is being developed. Gutiérrez-Jones (1995) addresses the questions raised by

MacKinnon in a different context, that is, in relation to Latinos: How do Latinos encounter state power? What is the law for Latinos? How does law work to legitimate the state, male [Anglo] power, itself? Can law do anything for Latinos? Can it do anything about Latino's status? Does how the law is used matter? (MacKinnon, 159) Because of organizations such as LULAC (League of United Latin American Citizens) and MALDEF (Mexican American Legal Defense Fund), the Chicano movement has dealt with the law in relation to Chicanos from its inception. What Gutiérrez-Jones shows is that the Latino is criminalized through the law.

Nevertheless, Chicana theorists can give us insight into what a new labor theory of value might be. Martinez and McCaughan base their argument on Wallerstein's world system theory. In their application of Wallerstein to the Chicana/Mexicana worker, this "transnational working class" is seen in relation to "the evolving capitalist world economy"(1990, 31). They refer to the migrant laborer in relation to his or her role in

> [p]art-time proletarian households: ". . . households who receive part of their life income from 'employers' or market-purchasers and part from direct production either by themselves or others (who may be kin). As a result, the full cost of reproduction is not borne by 'employers.' A good example would be the migrant laborer. A key question, however, is the degree to which they receive from their 'employers' a 'proportionate' share of the costs of reproduction. An example from Chicano/Mexicano history would be workers in the Bracero Program (Martínez and McCaughan, 32–33).

The transnational working class is "increasingly not limited by national boundaries, but is defined by the division of labor between two neighboring but unequal areas with the capitalist world-system," in this case, the United States and Mexico (1990, 34). This essay is very useful in developing a new value theory of labor insofar as it stresses the way in which Chicanas are undervalued both at the workplace and at home, at the way in which their work in the home is mystified as private labor for the husband. Hardt and Negri (1994) mention housework, along with the work of the nurse and the AIDS activist, as part of the use value which is not considered by capitalism and marxism.

Lourdes Arguelles (1990) describes the process of de-skilling and re-skilling of the female domestic worker in the United States and contrasts her life with the one she would have in Latin America. In Latin America, especially in rural areas, Arguelles argues, the domestic worker in the United States tries becomes part of the family. In the

United States, this is not the case. Arguelles states that when the domestic worker in the United States tries to participate in the family with her cooking, sewing, and other skills, she is told by her employer that these are too time-consuming. Instead, she is encouraged to learn to use technology in the cleaning of the house. A clear example of this can be found in the film *El Norte*. When Rosa tries, unsuccessfully, to use the washer and dryer, she is confused by the myriad of options and resorts to washing the family laundry by hand. She is told by the employer that she must use the appliances, because it is too much work to do the wash by hand. Rosa is becoming-cyborg; she has the emotion or affect that Hardt and Negri describe in their theory of affective labor and she is being socialized into developing the relationship to technology that Haraway (1991) describes.

Arguelles puts a forward a model that links socioeconomic analysis, political organizing and critical reflection. She describes a Tucson activist who made the connection between her situation in Mexico and her situation in the United States. Her analysis will become relevant towards the end of this essay because it puts forward a critical paradigm, the Chicana worker in relation to global economic shifts and her politicization in farmworker "circles" or discussion groups. This paradigm shares quite a bit with Haraway's cyborg and the ideas of Paulo Freire concerning organizing.

MacKinnon argues that feminism has been "schizoid" in its posture towards the state (1990, 160). On the one hand, it has taken a liberal approach and has supported state intervention if it could improve the status of women. A Marxist approach to the state has not been useful to women, she argues, because [Marxism] applied to women is always on the edge of counseling abdication of the state as an arena altogether—and with it those women whom the state does not ignore or who are in no position to ignore it (160)." Feminism's schizoid posture is understandable, given what women have endured under the auspices of the state. Some men have suffered in similar ways, but, according to MacKinnon, not due to the same relationship to the state. MacKinnon argues that women have suffered economic exploitation, and have been relegated to domestic slavery, forced into motherhood, sexually objectified, physically abused, used in denigration entertainment, deprived of a voice and authentic culture, disenfranchised and excluded from public life, subjected to physical insecurity, deprived of respect, credibility, and resources, silenced and denied public presence, voice and representation of their interests (160).

The treatment of women by the state overlaps in many ways with what Latinos have had done to them. MacKinnon distinguishes between the ways in which men dehumanize other men, ways which include enslavement, but not "socially as well as economically, prior to the operation of law, without express state acts, often in intimate contexts, as everyday life" (MacKinnon 1989,). She concludes that the state is male in the feminist sense. An analogous conclusion would be that the state is Anglo male, from the perspective of the Latino/a. From the perspective of the border dweller, the State is nationalist/ male.

From the perspective of the Latino, the state is Anglo male: "the state is male jurisprudentially, meaning that it adopts the standpoint of male power on the relation between law and society" (MacKinnon 163). Gutiérrez-Jones writes: "The state, of course, has a considerable investment in the psychological manipulation of behavior. Its legal institutions have participated in such conditioning by reinforcing the force/consent dichotomy and by giving apparent priority to the latter term in order to build the liberal ideal of voluntary participation in 'acceptable behavior. Force thus becomes the excluded term" (Gutiérrez-Jones 1995, 109).

Another feminist critic, Maria Mies, looks at the socialist state and the role which women play within it. She writes that in the building of the socialist state, the role of women in the role of nation-building is obscured by idealizing the founding fathers of the socialist state (199). She also attacks the distinction between the public and the private sphere, a distinction that she claims has been accepted by feminism (19). According to Mies, capitalism did not destroy the family; rather, with the help of the police and the state, it created it (1986, 105). The relegation of women to the family and the private or informal, subsidiary economy, ensures that "the 'big-men' are not challenged in their monopoly over state power" (1986, 199). She asks if women have more power than before after the creation of socialist states (1986, 177).

The second theory of the state that I will address is that of Uri Ra'anan. This theory is put forward in his discussion of the work of Karl Renner and Otto Bauer in an essay entitled "Nation and State: Order Out of Chaos" (Ra'anan et. al. 1991). Rather than addressing gender issues, Ra'anan attempts to create a model for the state in which ethnic conflicts can be resolved. He argues that, although this distinction is difficult in English, it is important to distinguish between state and nation. He uses the term *Staatsvolk* to distinguish between the ethnic group that created the state, is largely identified with it, constitutes the bulk of its elite, and is the source of the dominant culture, and the nation. In my reading of Negri's model, based on Spinoza, which will be discussed below, the *Staatsvolk* would consist of all ethnicities, not just one dominant one. In the U.S.-Mexico border region, Anglo-European culture plays the role of *Staatsvolk*. An example of a state being larger than a nation is Canada, Ra'anan argues, with two *Staatsvolk*, Anglophones and Francophones, each occupying a major region. He also refers to a 'Third Canada,' which consists of Indians, Inuit and others, including Danes, Germans, Dutch, Ukrainians, Italians, Jews, and Poles. An example of a nation larger than a state is Korea, which is divided into two states. There are also situations in which nations, such as the Hungarian as the Hungarian nation, exceed national boundaries. Although there is a Hungarian "state," thanks to frontiers imposed by World War I and II, nearly 3 million Magyars are excluded from what is now Hungary. This situation has something in common with that of Mexico, in which Mexico lost over one-half of its territory in the Mexican-American War. Although there is a Mexican "state," thanks to the Mexican-American War, a large part of the Mexican population now lives outside of Mexico. The border continues to divide families.

The discussion of the state is complicated by the relationship to nation. According to Ra'anan, confusion about the term "nation" leads to further confusion, in the West, surrounding the definition of citizenship:

> In any case, what many Western analysts simply do not seem to grasp is that their essentially territorial concept of nationality, according to which citizenship, loyalty to the nation and to the state are treated as interchangeable terms, may not be the accepted and that, both historically and at present, it has been and remains very much a minority view (Ra'anan *et. al.* 1991, 13).

Ra'anan's statement creates a space for the reconsideration of citizenship below. Ra'anan distinguishes the Western view from the Eastern view, which argues that a person's nationality is derived not from *jus solis* but rather from *jus sanguinis*, that is, cultural, religious, and historical identity, regardless of where he or she currently resides. Using the example of the Georgian living in Moscow, he explains that even if the Georgian speaks better Russian than his ancestral tongue, he/she still perceives him/herself to be Georgian. This is very similar to the Chicano, who may or may not speak Spanish, but still identifies him or herself in relation to Mexican and Chicano culture.

Another cultural phenomenon linked to the Eastern view that is shared by Chicanos/as is found in the following passage:

> Peoples whose state had disappeared from the map as a sovereign entity centuries earlier and whose national tongue had degenerated into a peasant dialect without a literature, being superseded as written and spoken forms of elite communication by the language of the conquerors, usually initiated their national renaissance by resuscitating their ancient language in modernized and literary form (Ra'anan *et. al.* 1991, 16).

Alurista (1977) and other writers have used the indigenous language Nahuatl in a similar manner. Ra'anan observes that it is the intelligentsia of the diaspora that form the center of such cultural movements, and this is certainly true in the case of Chicano culture. The Mexican diaspora could be defined as including both those of Mexican descent living in the United States and inhabitants of the United States who may have grown up in Mexico. Artists and writers originally from Mexico but now living in the United States. have participated in the formation of Chicano culture. Concomitant with this in the U.S.-Mexico border region is the situation of the Mixtec community. Along with other Mexicans, Mixtecs had been divided by the border. The Mixtec national anthem is taught to Mixtec children by their parents and the Mixtec language is the first language of the Mixtec community. Nahuatl is not only preserved in poetry written by intellectuals; it is the first language of many indigenous people in Mexico.

For Ra'anan, the problem of ethnicity and the state goes beyond language. There must also be a mechanism for conflict resolution which is provocative and suggestive. His model draws on both a Western, territorial definition of the state and the Eastern view of *jus sanguinis*, which appears in the model as a personal-ethnic definition. It has to do with three tiers and two groups. Country X is composed of two ethnic groups, the A's and the B's . . . at the lowest level—municipal and rural councils—the citizenry as a whole, irrespective of ethnic affiliation, would vote and be represented. At the intermediate level, the representative organs of the various ethnic associations, elected by their respective memberships, would act both as the territorial authorities in the autonomous regions or provinces where their own nationality constituted a majority, and as watchdogs and helpers in areas where their ethnic group was scattered in small numbers. Finally, at the highest level—central government—leading members of the various ethnic associations' representative organs would work together, with a functional division of tasks between them, leaving each nationality with the last word on those matters that were of particular concern to it. (Ra'anan *et. al.* 1991, 31)

What I find intriguing about Ra'anan's model is that it could be synthesized with a holographic model of the state, insofar as each part, in terms of ethnicity as well as territoriality, encapsulates the whole—not in linear representation from local, to state, to federal, but in a multidimensional manner. This holographic aspect, as an example of representative democracy, can lead us towards Spinoza's "good" City, which will be discussed below. In the intermediate and central government level, however, the territorial authorities and watchdogs and central government representatives would be forced to balance the needs of their own nationality and other nationalities. This differs from assimilation; it creates a stereoscopic viewpoint. Very simply, there could be A–Bs, in addition to the As and the Bs. Ra'anan deliberately leaves out the A–Bs, but I am inserting them into his model in order to look at the U.S.-Mexico border region in the metropolitan region of San Diego-Tijuana. The two "antagonistic" populations would be Anglo-Europeans and Mexicans. The A–Bs could be "border citizens" from either country who identified with both groups because of "social, marital and other assimilative processes" that had been at work to "blur the lines between" nationalities A and B.

I have discussed holography and border culture in *Border Writing* (1991). Briefly, the border dweller may see the object from more than one perspective due to exposure to at least two cultural/ethnic environments. Once this has occurred, the previous certainty about reality will be undermined. The border dweller has more in common with border dwellers in the other country than with the national government on either side of a border. A–Bs could include Chicanos/as, but probably not Chicano nationalists. A–Bs could also include Mexican-Americans, but probably not those whose primary identification was "American." However, with a new category of "border citizen" as an option, populations might shift in their affiliations. Another option for self-identification as a "border citizen" might be multiple citizenships.

This model brings us to the third theory of the state, Negri's, which I will discuss in relation to his notion of a fully constituted state. Kris Gutiérrez and McLaren (1997), refer to Hardt and Negri's analysis of the problem of liberalism and the postmodern state, which, they argue, can be summarized in the following terms:

The order and harmony and equilibrium of the system are achieved by excluding points of social conflict and insulating the system from social contents; tolerance means indifference to the determinations of social being and to the avoidance of social antagonisms; questions of labor, production, gender difference, racial difference, sexual orientation, desire, and value are discarded because they are considered personal, not political; the political system is based on absolute contingency rather than material determinations; society is self-referential and premised on *feasibility*, not desirability (1997, 215–16).

In this passage, it is clear that the multicultural educator must attend to all the questions to which the postmodern state is indifferent. Precisely because postmodern tolerance avoids social antagonisms, the questions of labor, production, gender difference, racial difference, sexual orientation, desire and value must be a focus in the multicultural classroom.

In their discussion of the paradoxes of the postmodern state, Hardt and Negri argue that representation is obsolete in postmodern society (1994, 271). Hardt and Negri discuss the term "constitution" in the following passage:

The methodology of constitution shares with the methodology of the liberal philosophical tradition a critique of the dialectical conception of totality, the linearity and teleology of historical development, the transcendental proposition of the common good, and the subsumption of individual and autonomous subjectivities in a centralized subject of authority. Perhaps the most important single tenet of liberal political theory is that the ends of society be indeterminate and thus that the movement of society remain open to the will of its constituent members" (1994, 286).

Hardt and Negri, however, offer a radical or constituent alternative to liberalism. They explain this alternative in ontological terms. Their discussion of ontology may be understood in a Foucauldian sense of our own historical ontology. In their attempt to explain their view of ontology, they refer to Martin Heidegger's being as a bringing forth, a revealing (*aletheia*) (1994, 287). As a democratic element in the encounter with the other, which may involve conflict, I understand Hardt and Negri to be offering Spinoza's common notion. They write: "When Spinoza defines the concept as a common notion, he affirms it as a construction of a means for knowing reality" (286). In this conceptual space, being can develop, or be brought forth from a first phase, *cupiditas* (the desire to live), to a second phase, "cooperation, love, and the incorporation with the living source of being" (286). I want to think about the common notion in a border region as a stereoscopic viewpoint or "means of knowing reality." The stereoscopic viewpoint can be understood as a midwife to the Heideggerean revealing, or bringing forth into being, discussed by Hardt and Negri. The links between the unpleasant encounter, conflict resolution, ethics and democracy are implied by Hardt and Negri in the following passage: "Ontology is a development of democracy and democracy is a line of conduct a practice of ontology" (285). Like the work of many Marxist theorists on the relationship between theory and praxis, this formulation involves simultaneous attention to both the epistemological and the ontological. The pedagogical implications of Hardt and Negri's statement bring us to Darder's (1991) call for the development of critical categories that can help the student to reclaim the conditions for a self-determined existence.

Negri is not only critical of capitalism but of marxism as well. In his view, a workerist perspective must replace the perspective of both Marxism and capitalism with regard to the worker as labor. Negri also discusses the rights state, which is characterized by its role as a guardian of individual rights. Very relevant to our discussion is his view that the convergence of right and law results in the disruption of social relationships (Hardt and Negri 1994, 82). His discussion of factory legislation is also relevant. Just as capitalism, according to Marx, requires factory legislation, we can extend this argument to school legislation, and more particularly, to Proposition 209. The implications of this analysis for our study are: education under capitalism can only be understood in relation to labor; a state mandate supporting education in fact supports the relationship of education to labor as waged labor. A theory of radical pedagogy calls for a social valorization of education not in relation to waged labor but for freedom.

Now, I want to extend the discussion of Spinoza's "good" City to Negri's vision of transitional socialism and to situate this vision of the border city. In Chapter 2, I discussed Spinoza's discussion of the relationship between affects and action, and his view that the transition from passivity to action takes place most efficiently in the city. Spinoza's "good" City, as described by Deleuze in *Expressionism in Philosophy*, "takes the place of reason for those who have none, and prepares, prefigures and its way imitates the work of reason. It is the City that makes possible the development of reason itself" (1992, 268). Spinoza's reason is linked to freedom. While the citizen in Spinoza's "good" City renounces rights personally, he or she preserves them in the civil state. Deleuze explains that for Spinoza, "the power of knowing, thinking and expressing one's thought remains an inalienable natural right" (1992, 267). For Spinoza, "nobody is born reasonable" and "Nobody is born a citizen" (Deleuze 1992, 259). In relation to education, a critical pedagogy could encourage this power of knowing, thinking and expressing. As the work of Adelaida R. Del Castillo suggests, a border dweller has the unique opportunity to become "reasonable" by virtue of being situated on cultural, linguistic, economic ,and other borders as a "citizen" because he or she participates, reasonably, in a community, regardless of country of birth. The border dweller being discussed here is neither a "*mestizo*" who signifies a "whitening" of a population, nor is he/she an "autonomous citizen who can fashionably choose whatever ethnic combinations [she/he] desires in order to reassemble [her/his] identity" (McLaren, 1997, 7). She is not a "metropolitan version of hybridity"; rather, she is a "postcolonial" hybrid, in Ragagopalan Radhakrishanan's (1996) terms. It is here, in the border dweller's capacity to become reasonable, that Negri's theory of the state and the multicultural state might overlap. That is, the "good" City could be part of the genealogy of the constituent subject in the postmodern state in that it could prepare and prefigure the way to reason in such a state.

　　To summarize the discussion of the state, we recall that in the works of MacKinnon, Ra'anan, and Hardt and Negri, there are different emphases in the critiques; in the first case, women are seen to suffer, in the second, ethnic minorities, and in the third all citizens to the extent that the state is not fully constituted. These critics all find much lacking in the liberal state. MacKinnon's critique of the state from a feminist perspective is suggestive of ways the state could be theorized in relation to Latinos. Ra'anan's model of the multi-ethnic state is closest to Hardt and Negri's in that it focused on the problem of non-identity and conflict. However, the model remained, at least in most aspects, in the realm of a representative democracy. Hardt and Negri formulate the problem of the state and democracy differently, using the term "fully constituted."

　　This discussion of the state leads us to current research on citizenship. Both Adelaida R. Del Castillo and Meehan discuss a new kind of citizenship. In *Citizenship and the European Community*, Meehan writes:

> It is that a new kind of citizenship is being relocated to a new level. It is that a new kind of citizenship is emerging that is neither national nor cosmopolitan but that is multiple in the sense that identities, rights and obligations, associated by Heater (1990) with citizenship, are expressed through an in-

creasingly complex configuration of common Community institutions, states, national and transnational voluntary associations, regions and alliances of regions (1993, 1).

Del Castillo argues that the definition of citizenship is undergoing a change in the United States and that this change can be seen in the communities built among migrant women workers from Mexico. In California, a state in which the legal status of certain students has been debated recently, the situation of the migrant worker is widely discussed in the media. Human rights activists Roberto Martínez, Director of the American Friends Service Committee in San Diego, and Victor Clark, in Tijuana, along with community activists and artists, including members of the Border Arts Workshop/*Taller de arte fronterizo* (BAW-TAF), have fought to protect the human rights of undocumented workers, regardless of their legal status.

Meehan argues that the notion of citizenship has changed over time and that there is an overlap between political, legal and social rights. She also mentions the historical factor in such discussions. In the border region, the legal definition of a citizen has changed over time and the rights of noncitizens have also changed: Legal rights have been in question while some political and social rights have been exercised. Gloria Anzaldúa addresses these historical changes as they relate to Mexicans in *Borderlands* (1987). Meehan argues, following Bryan Turner (1986), that we should "unravel" legal status nationality (Meehan 1993, 8).

Meehan reminds us that "in Aristotle's self-governing community, citizenship meant membership of a community where assets were distributed so that all had in interest in contributing to as well as benefiting" (1993, 26). Unlike eighteenth-century thinkers, Aristotle discussed "communality and conviviality" whereas the former were interested in "individualism connected to economic rights" (Meehan 1993, 26). Many have argued in the border region that undocumented workers contribute greatly, through their labor and their taxes, and therefore deserve to benefit, in the form of education and social services.

In terms of benefits in the European context, Meehan shows the many conflicting definitions of who is insured and who is covered by social assistance for workers and their families. Unlike the situation in California, in which migrant workers face continual discrimination and cutbacks in social services, in the European Community, the Court has been committed, in areas which overlap with Raymond Aaron's civil, political and human rights, to the protection of those rights for migrant workers. For example, "migrants count as workers if not fully employed . . . and even if their travel is not connected with work" (Meehan, 89).

Meehan looks to Carole Pateman's work, in which Patemen argues that "it is not possible to realize women's citizenship in the context of contractual theories" (Meehan 1988, 104). She explains that Pateman bases this argument on her view that "since women were brought into civil society under the tutelage and sexual domination of men, the political contract was among brothers, not human beings" (Meehan 1988, 104). In Hardt and Negri's vision of the state, social bonds, community and citizenship are created through joyful work in which the postmodern subjects combine technological knowledge and care. The harbingers of this new subjectivity, nurses, AIDS activists and transnational working women, create this civil society rather than be-ing brought into it under the domination of men.

The second example of new definitions of citizenship is the work of Kymlicka. Kymlicka discusses: (1) the politics of multiculturalism; (2) individual rights and collective rights; (3) the liberal tradition in rela-tion to the claims of multiculturalism; (4) individual freedom, particu-larly in illiberal cultures; (5) the role of the state, justice and minority rights; (6) political representation and minority voices; (7) the limits of toleration in the liberal state; (8) sources of unity in a democratic multination state. Of these, of particular interest with regard to specu-lation about a theory of the state based on border culture are: (1) the role of the state, justice and minority rights, a topic which is also dealt with at length by Gutiérrez-Jones (1995); (2) the politics of multiculturalism and (3) sources of unity in a democratic multination state. Kymlicka's chapter "Justice and Minority Rights" treats the top-ics of the equality argument, the role of historical agreements, the value of cultural diversity, and the analogy of states. The equality ar-gument is very relevant in relation to affirmative action and education. While "in many cases claims for group-specific rights are simply an attempt by one group to dominate and oppress another," another passage on "some groups" could be applied to the situation of the Chicano/a:

Some groups are unfairly disadvantaged in the cultural market-place . . . Group differentiated rights—such as territorial autonomy, veto powers, guaranteed representation in central institutions, land claims and language rights—can help rectify this disadvantage (1995, 109).

Against Kymlicka's is the prevailing view in California, where the English the Official Language movement continues to gain support and Proposition 209 has been defeated. In the Southwest, the most important historical agreement for Chicanos/as is the Treaty of Guadalupe Hidalgo. As Kymlicka points out, the language rights guaranteed Chicanos by this treaty were ignored as soon as an anglophone majority settled in the region.

Kymlicka is skeptical about the defense of cultural diversity as being in the best interests of the whole society. He finds this argument to be weaker than the equality argument described above in terms of unfair advantage or the historical argument. His view is interesting in relation to the emphasis that the educational system in the United States places on the value of cultural diversity. Proponents of multicultural education need to address such skepticism. One way to do this is to extend the discussion of Kymlicka's liberal state into a discussion of the postmodern state.

The third study of citizenship I will consider is that of Spinner. While I have focused in this study on multiracial, multiethnic, multilingual inhabitants of border regions, with multiple citizenships and multiple nationalities in a postmodern state, Spinner, in *The Boundaries of Citizenship* (1994) looks at race, ethnicity, nationality, and language in relation to citizenship in a liberal, democratic state. Rather than putting forward a theory of the liberal state, Spinner shows how cultural identity is affected by the tensions surrounding equality and individual rights. He chooses to discuss liberal democratic states, and uses the United States as an example of such a state, while conceding that much of what occurs in the United States is illiberal (Spinner 1994, 11). Spinner also concedes that a limitation of liberal thought in some cases has been its blindness to issues of race, ethnicity, and nationality. He uses the example of John Jay, in the Federalist Papers, who is grateful for America's homogeneity: the same ancestors, language, religion, view of government and culture. Spinner rightly observes that this view ignores Blacks, Native Americans, Jews, and those from countries other than Britain (1994, 9).

There are four insights in Spinner's book that are relevant to this study. The first is that the meanings of race, ethnicity and nationality are contested, but that this does not mean that any identity can be created (1994, 29). The second is that liberalism has a complex relationship to cultural differences and to nationalism. This is significant in relation to the U.S.-Mexico border. Spinner explains that, on the one hand, in order to maintain distinct cultural groups, boundaries must be maintained. On the other hand, liberal citizenship and equality call for a breaking down or crossing of boundaries (1994, x). Spinner points out that it is this breaking down of boundaries that results in nationalist movements in liberal societies. This model could be applied to the U.S.-Mexico border in relation to the Chicano movement. The Chicano movement in its nationalist period, as discussed in Chapter 1, existed, and to some extent continues to exist, in a state of tension *vis-à- vis* liberal society, in this case, the United States. What Spinner does not address is a border identity that is neither nationalist nor assimilationist.

The next two points have to do with Spinner's sensitivity to the subtleties and complexities of ethnicity. Spinner extends Benedict Anderson's view of nation, that the nation is both limited and imagined. He observes that similarly, one's ethnicity is both limited (or as I understand him bounded) and imagined (1994, 27). His respect for ethnic differences make him skeptical of Richard Rorty's simplistic solution to unpleasant encounters between people: "'All you need is the ability to control your feelings when people who strike you as irredeemably different show up . . .'" (quoted in Spinner). For Spinner, there is too great a distance between Rorty's suggestion of duplicity and Aristotle's demand that "in order to become just," "one must perform just acts" (1994, 48). Spinner appears to be calling for an actual ability to treat the other with respect, rather than Rorty's suggestion that we pretend to like each other (46). Regarding Rorty, Hardt and Negri write:

> In Rorty's hands . . . the realization of Rawl's tolerant system becomes dependent on its indifference to and avoidance of social conflicts. Postmodern liberal tolerance is thus based not on the inclusion but actually the exclusion of social differences (Hardt and Negri 1994, 236).

Spinoza's call to transform passive, negative emotions as responses to unpleasant encounters into joyful emotions in response to pleasant encounters, described in great detail in the *Ethics*, provides an alternative to Rorty's facile solution to urban conflicts.

Spinner spends little time on the topic of multicultural education, although he does point to problems encountered by the New York Social Studies Review and Development Committee (1991). In his view, the goals of the committee and of many advocates of multicultural education are confused. In his own discussion of multicultural education, however, he himself makes potentially conflicting statements, such as, "Teachers should not be teaching their students to take pride in illiberal aspects of different cultures" and "History should not be taught in a way that denigrates or ignores some groups and celebrates others" (Spinner 1994, 178–179). Multicultural education in the postmodern era must be conceived within a context that goes beyond the liberal state in order to circumvent this unsatisfactory outcome of Spinner's critique.

To summarize this discussion of citizenship, we recall that in all of the critics considered, Meehan, Kymlicka, and Spinner, there was attention to ethnicity and nationality in relation to the full rights of citizenship. Of the three, the most significant for this discussion was Meehan's new definition of citizenship as multiple in terms of identities, rights, and obligations. In the context of globalization and the postmodernist state, and particularly in relation to the U.S.-Mexico border, this view, shared by Del Castillo and Heater, is visionary. While Kymlicka rejected the "good of the society" as the most effective argument in defending multiculturalism, he conceded that in some cases, the state might use the following as forms of rectification: territorial autonomy, veto powers and guaranteed representation in central institutions, land claims, and language. Unfortunately, if we apply one of these forms of rectification, representation in educational institutions, at the time of this writing, we find that in California, the guaranteed representation in institutions of higher learning is being dismantled. Spinner explained the complex relationship that the liberal state has to ethnic differences and nationalism. Like Hardt and Negri, Spinner found Rorty's solution to urban conflicts in a multicultural society be unsatisfactory. While attempting to discuss multiculturalism in education, Spinner's own contradictory conclusions raised a dilemma about respecting illiberal cultures. A response to this is suggested by considering these three critics together. In a state in which, first, citizenship would be redefined in terms of multiple citizenships; second, some of the suggestions of Kymlicka could be supported; and third, Spinner's careful analyses of various ethnic communities could be considered, the dichotomy liberal/illiberal would be irrelevant, because we would be leaving the realm of the liberal state and entering the realm of the postmodern state.

Education may be seen as a crucial link between the citizen and democracy, and I will now turn to a discussion of critical pedagogy. I will look at Jameson's use of Hegel (1807) and Darder's use of Frankfurt Theory, Foucault, and Freire. It is my intention to reveal certain contradictions in the canon debates and critical pedagogy that serve to undermine the very laudable projects of opening up the canon and bringing critical theory into the classroom. In the previous sections on the state and citizenship, labor and theories of value entered into the debates considered. What is needed, as much as a value theory of labor and a labor theory of value is a pedagogical theory of the State; proceeding from such a theory, the role of education and the importance of the control of rhetorical options could be addressed more easily. As mentioned earlier, in Gutiérrez-Jones's discussion of Guillory's "Canonical and Non-canonical: A Critique of the Current Debate," Gutiérrez-Jones explains how the "strength institutions exhibit over time rests on a sum total of complex practices which displace potentially disruptive rhetorical options by formally prohibiting such disruptive practices" (1995, 11). Another essay that addresses canon debates in literature is Fredric Jameson's "Third World Literature in the Era of Multicultural Capitalism" (1986).

As valuable as Fredric Jameson's work is in reconceptualizing the literary canon and developing a critical pedagogy, in "Third World Literature in the Era of Multinational Capitalism," there is a problem in the Hegelian argumentation when considered from a Deleuzo-Guattarian (1986) perspective. According to Ahmad, in addition to having problems placing Jameson in a "world" when Ahmad rejects the three worlds theory, he finds Jameson's work to be a determined by a gendered and a "racial milieu" (Ahmad 1987). The evidence of the assumed milieu, according to Ahmad, is that he finds himself to be excluded from it when Jameson distinguishes between First World and other readers.

Any model that hopes to capture the U.S.-Mexico border must address a gendered and racial milieu that is inclusive and must be attentive to elements of the Third World in the First World and vice versa. The role of Hegel in contemporary criticism, although a focus of Derrida's, is often complex and contradictory. Jameson, who also refers to Foucault, at the same time uses the Hegelian dialectic in his argument, without noting points where Foucault's and Hegel's work cannot be conflated. Jameson writes, in a passage quoted by Ahmad, that Hegel's analysis of lordship and bondage in the *Phenomenology* "may still be the most effective way" to "dramatize" the first world/third world relationship:

Two equals struggle each for recognition by the other: the one is willing to sacrifice life for this supreme value. The other, a heroic coward in the Brechtian,

Schweykian sense of loving the body and the material world too well, gives in, in order to continue life. The Master—now the fulfillment of a baleful and inhuman feudal-aristocratic disdain for life without honor—proceeds to enjoy the benefits of his recognition by the other, now become his humble serf or slave. But at this point two distinct and dialectically ironic reversals take place: only the Master is now genuinely human, so that "recognition" by this hence forth sub-human form of life which is the slave evaporates at the moment of its attainment and offers no genuine satisfaction. 'The truth of the Master,' Hegel observes grimly, 'is the Slave, while the truth of the Slave, on the other hand, is the Master.' But a second reversal is in process as well; for the slave is called upon to labor for the master and to furnish him with all the material benefits befitting his supremacy. But this mean that, in the end only the slave knows what reality and resistance of matter really are; only the slave can attain some true materialistic consciousness of his situation, since it is precisely to that that he is condemned (Jameson 1986, 85).

In his critique, Ahmad points out that this reduction of the relationship between the two cultural logics of the First and Worlds to Hegel is problematic. While Jameson defines the first and second worlds in terms of their production systems, that is, capitalism and socialism, he defines the third world in terms of

> . . . an 'experience' of externally inserted phenomena . . . Ideologically this classification divides the world between those who make history and those who are mere objects of it; elsewhere in the text, Jameson would significantly re-invoke Hegel's famous description of the master/slave relation to encapsulate the first/third world opposition (Ahmad 1987, 6–7).

In other words, just by referring to the Third World as the slave, and the First World as the master, the economic role of the Third World to the First and Second is not addressed and the Third World remains undefined, or in Ahmad's term, "in a limbo" from a marxist perspective (1987, 7). Of course, Ahmad is not the first to have raised these issues; Leninists and their critics have struggled since the Russian Revolution to theorize how and when socialism might arise and in which countries. In fact, Mies not only questions whether or not the Leninist model is appropriate for non-European countries; she asks if it is even appropriate for European countries. What Ahmad is pointing out, however, is that it is not helpful to use a model, in this case Hegel's master-slave relation, that omits entire populations of the world.

In Hardt and Negri's formulation of the contemporary version of this problem, it is no longer a question of where socialism might arise, but one "where both the crisis of capitalism and the end of socialist transition" are relevant" (308). I am extending their argument to bor-

der regions, not because they produce revolutionary subjects necessarily, but because they exist between the crisis of capitalism and the
end of socialist transition. This formulation describes quite well those
regions between Eastern and Western Europe. It is the backdrop against
which NAFTA negotiations were conducted and the Chiapas uprising
occurred.

To summarize this discussion of Jameson, despite his intention, to
open the canon to include a culturally diverse body of texts, the Hegelian
model on which he relied omitted, or at least left in limbo, entire
populations. Ahmad finds himself put in the position of Cornelius
May, neither African nor European, when Jameson makes him the
Other (Turner 1986, 1992). However, Ahmad refuses this position
along with its attendant Hegelian argumentation.

Darder links her notion of critical pedagogy to Frankfurt Theory,
Foucault and Freire. Her work, which refers to Giroux's (1991) and S.
Warren's (1994) definitions of the dialectic, gives us an opportunity to
link some aspects of critical pedagogy to Adorno's negative dialectic
(1973) and to Foucault (1984) while still noting important differences.
Darder discusses dialectic thought as a process that seeks out social
contradictions. She states that knowledge, power, and domination are
linked from the perspective of dialectical thought (1991, 82). There is
some ambiguity about what she means by dialectical thought, since
she does not refer to Marx by name; but she does state that her definition comes from Adorno. Given Freire's centrality in critical pedagogy, her definition is most certainly informed by his work as well.
Although I will raise questions about critical pedagogy's use of the
term "dialectical" in the following section, it is in the spirit of clarification; my intention is to suggest that it is negative dialectical theory
that can allow us to see how knowledge, power and domination are
linked in a multicultural environment.

Darder makes the very important argument that a revolutionary
pedagogy calls for a radical restructuring of the society which goes on
outside of the classroom. Here, I would agree with Darder. While she,
along with other critical pedagogues, grounds her philosophical perspective in what she calls a critical perspective, however, that term
has been used refer to several traditions, with important differences
within and between them. For example, although Adorno was a member of the Frankfurt School, his theory of negative dialectics is not to
be conflated with Marx's dialectic, as Gillian Rose argues in her study
of Adorno, *The Melancholy Science* (1978). Conflicting philosophi-

cal positions coexist in the discourse of critical pedagogy and in Darder's work.

Foucault's work, which is central in Darder's, can lead us to a vision of radical restructuring of society. In their discussion of the fully constituted state, Hardt and Negri refer to Foucault: "To recognize this constitutive alternative we must begin with what Foucault calls a historical ontology of ourselves, a genealogy of the constitution of social being, by asking how we are constructed as subjects of knowledge, how we are constituted as subjects of power, how are we constituted as moral subjects of action (Foucault, "What is Enlightenment" 45–49, quoted in Hardt and Negri 1994, 286). I refer to the notion of our own historical ontology earlier in this chapter in the section on Negri's theory of the state. There are many passages in Darder's *Culture and Power* that address the question of the construction of the student as a subject of knowledge and power; what she does not do clearly is to attend to the philosophical assumptions of Hegel in relation to Foucault, nor do other leading theorists of critical pedagogy. In the reading I am putting forward in this chapter, Foucault is arguing for a positive, not a negative view of power. This view is related to his anti-Hegelian stance. For the purposes of critical pedagogy, as opposed to consistent philosophical argumentation, it may be that the power as positive vs. power as negative dichotomy, like process vs. skills in the teaching of writing, is not a useful place to draw battle lines. Perhaps, as Delpit (1995) argues with regard to process vs. skills, both are useful in a multicultural classroom. Furthermore, regardless of underlying Hegelian assumptions, the stated arguments in the discourse of critical pedagogy focus on power as positive force rather than as merely repressive. This is clear in Darder's discussion of Foucault and power (1991, 27).

Following Giroux (1993), Darder collapses Adorno and the Marxist dialectic when she discusses the dialectic and the negative dialectic. She quotes Giroux:

Critical theorists argue that what is needed to unravel the source, mechanism, and elements that constitute the fabric of school culture is a theory of dialectical critique. Based on Adorno's (1973) notion of negative dialectics, it begins with a rejection of traditional representations of reality. The underlying assumption is that critical reflection is formed out of the principles of negativity, contradiction, and mediation. This calls for a thorough interrogation of all universal "truths" and social practices that go unquestioned in schools because they are concealed in the guise of objectivity and neutrality (Giroux, 1983, n.p., quoted in Darder 1991, 82).

While I would agree that Adorno does problematize identity theory, A=A, which he and Derrida both argue is fundamental in Western thought, and in this way might be said to reject traditional representations of reality, I would take issue with the view that there is a simple and obvious relationship between "the principles of negativity, contradiction and mediation" and Adorno's theory of nonidentity. In his discussion of labor as a bourgeois category and the dialectic, Negri explains the relationship between the dialectic (negativity, contradiction, and mediation) and the conflict. Hegel's dialectic is dead, according to Negri, which we can see if we apply it to a state in which productive labor, itself born in the modern factory, imposes the model of the factory on the entire society, and the contradiction is not annulled but multiplied. For Negri, the workerist critique is not dialectical; rather, it is focused on the conflict. Negri criticizes Marxism for reducing the complexity of the worker to the role to which the worker was condemned as labor in capitalist society. Rose writes that "[although] Adorno retains an Hegelian vocabulary—subject, object, mediation— his reception of Hegel's philosophy is structured by his reception of Nietzsche's philosophy as well as that of Marx. . . . Adorno's criticism of identity thinking means that he has rejected an Hegelian notion of the subject as the unity of the universal and the particular." (Rose 1978, 55). In other words, Adorno's dialectic cannot be reduced to Marx's (55). We might conclude here, that in the context of critical pedagogy, as in the previous discussion of skills and process, perhaps the nullification vs. the multiplication of the contradiction distinction is an opposition over which it is not productive to draw battle lines. I would like, however, to link the notion of the multiplication of the contradiction to Delpit's discussion of power.

Delpit writes that "those with power are frequently least aware of— or least willing to acknowledge—its existence. Those with less power are often most aware of its existence" (1995, 26). Negri is critical of the way in which both capitalism and Marxism define the individual in terms of labor, despite Marxism's stated intention of freeing the worker. The analogy related to Delpit's observation would be that both the unveiled power of the traditional, hierarchical classroom and the veiled, understated power of the progressive classroom may have negative results for a student not aware of middle class norms of behavior. Following Negri, who writes as an anarchist critical of marxism, we might say that just as the workerist critique is not dialectical, but rather focused on the conflict, so a truly multicultural critical pedagogy is not

dialectical, but rather, focused on the nonidentity in Adorno's negative dialectic. How might we imagine an application of this in the
classroom? Delpit's critique of the progressive educator's downplaying
of power consists in revealing that rather than truly creating a democratic classroom, it creates a classroom in which African-American
boys are stigmatized. Delpit explains that "if veiled commands are
ignored, the child will be labeled a behavior problem and possibly
officially classified as behavior disordered" (1995, 34). Ironically, the
white progressive teacher, with the best of intentions, might unwit-
tingly participate in such a system of cultural misunderstanding. My
purpose in this discussion of the dialectic is to point out that that even
such a seemingly innocuous term in the progressive community such
as "dialectical" should be looked at critically.

In short, I reject the implication that negative dialectics should be
used interchangeably with dialectics. Rather, we should follow Rose's
linking of nonidentity and critical thought. If we do this, we can ob-
serve the nuances in Adorno's analysis that are lost in the passages of
Giroux considered here. Adorno presents conflicting theses, such as,
in some passages, that consciousness has become completely reified
and, in other passages, that consciousness is becoming increasingly
reified. Adorno raises issues about the relationship between theory
and practice in the context of his discussion of negative dialectics. He
discusses theory in relation to the concept:

> Theory . . . must transform the concept which, as it were, brings in from
> outside into those which the object has by itself, into that which the object
> would itself like to be, and confront it with what it is (quoted in Rose 44).

Rose clarifies these issues by delineating three ways of thinking discussed by Adorno: (1) identity thinking; (2) non-identity thinking and
(3) rational identity thinking (Rose 1978, 44). It is in nonidentity thinking that one is able to see that "given the present state of society (the
capitalist mode of production), the concept cannot identify its true
object" (Rose 1978, 44). She develops this idea in the following passage: "To confront . . . present society, with what 'it is', that is, to
compare it with the condition of its rational identity, is to see the nonidentity in the relation between the concept and the object" (44). The
concept, as a focal point, is not just a philosophical interest for Adorno;
as Rose states in the introduction, "Concepts, as ordinarily used, are
distorting and mask social reality" (10). Here, Derrida and Adorno are
quite close in that both call for an inquiry into the philosophical as-

sumptions of the concept. In Derrida's case, it is clear that even Marxism's concepts must be interrogated.

My objection to Giroux's (1991) use of Adorno is that he does not clarify the relationship between the Frankfurt School and Marxism. More specifically, he does not pay enough attention to the aspects in Adorno which call for Marxism to turn the negative dialectic on its own dialectical approach. Rose explains the way in which Adorno's negative dialectical approach both resembles and differs from Marx's:

> Thus Adorno does not accept Marx's ideas as an *a priori* theory of society, but *presents a dialectic*: he shows how various modes of cognition, Marxist and non-Marxist, are inadequate and distorting when taken in isolation; and how by confronting them with each other precisely on the basis of an awareness of their individual limitations, they may nevertheless yield insight into social processes (Rose 1978, 51).

The Marxist dialectical view, which Darder takes from Warren, she expresses as follows: "It begins with the fact of human existence and the contradictions and disjunctions that, in part, shape it and make problematic its meaning in the world" (Darder 1991, 80). She then quotes McLaren in a passage that describes how the educator could help the student see "the problems of society as more than simply isolate events of individuals or deficiencies in the social structure. Rather, these problems are part of the interactive context between the individual and society" (McLaren, quoted in Darder 1991, 81). Darder explains that "Dialectical thought seeks out these social contradictions and sets up a process of open and thoughtful questioning that requires reflection to ensue back and forth between the parts and the whole, the object and the subject, knowledge and human action, process and product, so that further contradictions may be discovered (81). Darder concludes:

> Hence, the primary purpose of a dialectical critique within the context of a critical pedagogy is to address two concerns: (1) the linking of social experiences with the development of modes of criticism that can interrogate such experiences and reveal both their strengths and weaknesses; and (2) the presentation of a mode of praxis fashioned in new critical thought aimed at reclaiming the conditions of self-determined existence (82).

Before leaving this discussion of Frankfurt theory and Darder, there is one more complication that must be considered. In order not to miss another nuance of Adorno's, an addendum must be added to the overlap between Foucault's attention to nonidentity and Adorno's negative dialectic. The vision of affirmation and joy, put forward by Hardt and Negri and very much a part of their understanding of Foucault's dictum that we ask how we are constructed as subjects of knowledge, is grounded in Nietzsche. Nietzschean affirmation is suspect in the view of Adorno, as evidenced by the conclusion of "The Essay as Form" in *Notes on Literature* (1991) in which he writes that even the essay distrusts Nietzschean affirmation.

Playing an even greater role in Darder's work than Frankfurt Theory is Freire. Darder refers to Freire's notion of praxis, that humans are "beings of praxis," unlike animals, and that "men [and women] . . . create the realm of nature and history . . . It is as transforming and creating beings that men, in their permanent relations with reality, produce" (Freire 1970, 90–91, quoted in Darder 83). What is debatable is how this union of theory and praxis is to occur. While some Marxists accept a notion of political consciousness that has its roots in Hegelian consciousness, Deleuze does not. Further work needs to be done by critical pedagogues to differentiate Freire's notion of *conscientizaçao* from Hegelian consciousness. In his book *Gilles Deleuze: an Apprenticeship in Philosophy* (1993), Hardt discusses the master-slave dialectic. He writes: "Hegel's slave is interested in consciousness and independence; he is too preoccupied with his death and too busy thinking about his work to posit the question of value . . . Deleuze . . . wants to have nothing to do with self-consciousness and the self it gives rise to. . . . Along with Nietzsche he [Deleuze] views it as a sickness, a ressentiment caused by the reflection of a force back into itself. What Deleuze is searching for, instead, is a productive exteriority which is based on affirmation" (Hardt 1993, 62).

Just as certain philosophical problems are raised by Darder's reliance on Frankfurt Theory, there are also controversial philosophical assumptions in the work of Freire. An important critique of Freire in relation to the role of teachers comes from Roberto Rivera (1992), who discusses the problems inherent in the concept of [political] consciousness. He begins his critique by examining liberation theology. Rivera is critical of liberation theology discourses because they borrow sometimes self-defeating discursive strategies. He argues that Freire borrows two such strategies, intentionality and philosophical authority. Rivera objects to Freire's uncritical use of Husserl and specifically to his use of an image that is found in Husserl's *Ideas*, In this image, the European philosopher is seated at his desk, observing the items in his study.

In addition to Rivera's critique, Freire has been accused of, as in Aronowitz' summary of his work in *Dead Artists, Live Writers*, "reproducing the Leninist dictum according to which the task of the avant-garde intellectuals—in this case teachers—is to lead the masses into liberation" (Aronowitz 1994, 226). Against this view, Aronowitz focuses on Freire's call for workers, the exploited, and the oppressed, to "share their power over knowledge, share the power to shape the future" (226). Here, Freire is closer to Foucault. Foucault, Freire, and Darder, although by different routes, reach similar conclusions, as can be seen if we recall the task Foucault has set for us—"a genealogy of the constitution of social being... how we are constructed as subjects of knowledge, how we are constituted as subjects of power, how are we constituted as moral subjects of action"—and the numerous passages in Darder's *Culture and Power* that address the question of the construction of the student as a subject of knowledge and power (Hardt and Negri 1994, 286).

To summarize this discussion of Darder, her goal of teaching students to see how they are constituted as subjects of power does not rely on Hegelian philosophical assumptions; rather, it is a Foucauldian goal. Whether or not she explicitly makes the argument, we can work backwards from Foucault and link her to Negri's project. However, we must not collapse the differences between Nietzsche and Adorno. At best, we can find conflicting strands in Darder's project which may on the surface appear Foucauldian, but upon closer examination, raise unresolved philosophical issues.

We have seen that theories of value and labor in a multi-ethnic/feminist state, citizenship in a multiethnic/feminist state, and a critical pedagogy for a multicultural classroom that is suggested by this chapter share elements of Mies, MacKinnon, Foucault, Freire, Negri, and Darder, among others. Hegel's dialectic is less useful than Marx and Adorno's, despite Marxist Jameson's reference to it, in understanding First World-Third World relations. Kymlicka shows the limits of the liberal state towards ethnic minorities, while Mies shows the limits of the socialist state towards both women and ethnic minorities. That Kymlicka understands the limits of the liberal state towards ethnic minorities does not lead him to the conclusion that cultural diversity is in the best interests of the society, or at least, that this is as strong an argument for cultural diversity that could be made, such as the historical one. What Kymlicka seems to be missing is that cultural diversity exists in a postmodern society and that the definition of "best interests" must be redefined. If "in the best interests" is to be linked to democracy, then both the historical and the "best interests" argument can be made. Although there is no theory of the Chicano state, Gutiérrez-Jones is able to show how the state criminalizes Chicanos, as MacKinnon shows how the state affects women. Meehan has opened up the definition of citizenship beyond nationality, as has Del Castillo.

Darder and Hardt and Negri overlap in that their projects are Foucauldian. A shared concern is that of "asking how we are constructed as subjects of knowledge, how we are constituted as subjects of power, how we are constituted as moral subjects of action" (Hardt and Negri 1994, 287). For Darder, a critical pedagogy allows this inquiry to take place in the classroom. Nietzsche is the common element in the work of Adorno, Negri, Foucault, Deleuze and Guattari and Anzaldúa. This is obvious in the work of Negri, Foucault and Deleuze and Guattari. It is less obvious in the work of Adorno and Anzaldúa. It is the affirmation of difference in the work of Adorno, found in his theory of negative dialectics, which signals one example of Nietzshe's influence. In Anzaldúa 's there is also an affirmation of difference in her figure of the border dweller, whose identity cannot be encompassed completely by categories on either side of the border. In their reference to Foucault, Hardt and Negri, also overlap with Darder when they base their theory of a Spinozian democratic state on "a historical ontology of ourselves, a genealogy of the constitution of social being" (Hardt and Negri 1994, 287).

In the following section I want to take the reader on a journey from seeking out social contradictions, a goal of critical pedagogy, to a model of a feminist, multicultural, multi-ethnic, post-national, postmodern state. This journey will include: (1) a description of the multicultural state; (2) a discussion of theoretical and pedagogical links between critical pedagogy and the multicultural state; (3) an exploration of strategies for the radical restructuring of society; (4) an analysis of the ethical components of the "good" classroom as it relates to the multicultural state; and (5) attention to the implications of bicultural pedagogy for border theory and vice versa.

The first stop of this journey is a description of the multicultural state. What would the multicultural state look like? This state would be fully constituted by the multitude. Hardt and Negri write that in their model of the state, "the one is really the multitude and the life of the multitude is democracy" (1994, 311). The multitude would include women, men, bisexuals, lesbians, people with mental illnesses, and a multiplicity of ethnicities. No group would be singled out to be criminalized. Hardt and Negri continue: "The republic and law itself are thus reduced to procedure" (311). This state would extend beyond national boundaries. Can we imagine a state in which "chance" encounters, characterized by violence and fear, could be replaced by organized, joyful encounters among gays, lesbians, bisexuals, undocumented workers, HIV-positive citizens, the homeless, African-Americans, Latinos, Asians and white heterosexual males? In this state, the category of documented or not would be irrelevant, because citizenship would be redefined and would be based on participation in communities that crossed national boundaries. On the "plane of consistency," or the environment, there would exist the possibility of organized, pleasant encounters, not just accidental, unpleasant ones. Regarding this plane, Deleuze writes that on this multicultural, multigendered, multiethnic "common plane of immanence on which all bodies, all minds and all individuals are situated . . . there is no longer a subject, but only individuating affective states of an anonymous force" (Deleuze 1988, 128).

The second stop of this journey, which will consist of four brief forays, has to do with the theoretical and pedagogical links between the state and critical pedagogy. What would be the relationship of critical pedagogy to the state? What kinds of interactions could occur in the classroom that would prepare citizens to live in the "good" or border city? What opportunities for organized encounters could occur in the multicultural classroom as opposed to the "good" or border city? What example of the common notion could we imagine in a classroom situation?

First, we will consider what the relationship of critical pedagogy to the state would be. Critical pedagogy would be the link between the fully constituted state and the multicultural classroom. It would play an important part in bringing this state into being. According to Darder, school is an "apprenticeship in democracy" (1991, 65). It is an environment in which the habit of submission can be changed through critical thought. For Darder, taking a phrase from Dewey (1916), critical pedagogy is a kind of "deconstructing the 'fear of intercourse with others'" (64–65). I understand her to mean that the distinctions between nonfear and fear, as well as self and other, are to be exposed as hierarchies. In addition, the distinctions are to be undermined and revealed to be unstable. What Darder refers to as a deconstruction of fear is described by Spinoza as becoming reasonable, which for him means developing the ability to organize pleasant encounters with others and to perceive and comprehend what we have in common with others (Deleuze 1988, 5–57). These abilities will result in the transformation of inaction to action. For Spinoza, the individual can be said to be free when in possession of the power of acting. The power of acting is made possible by transforming sad passions into joy-affects. For Spinoza, the tyrant and the oppressed are united in their hatred and resentment of life (Deleuze 1998, 25). Therefore, the individual is as willing to fight to defend an oppressive system as s/he is for freedom (25). Education can provide, according to Dewey, "'a large variety of shared undertakings' and experiences" to prevent the master/slave dichotomy in the education of some students being trained to be managers and other workers" (Dewey 1916, 84–85, quoted in Darder 1988, 64).

Second, what kinds of interactions could occur in the multicultural, "good" classroom to prepare citizens to live in the "good" or border city? Successful living in the "good" or border city would be the ability to be reasonable in Spinoza's sense, that is, to organize pleasant encounters and to perceive and comprehend common notions. Robert Hurley explains that for Spinoza, interacting with things and understanding things cannot be separated. Therefore, the "unit of understanding" is not "the form or function or organism," but rather "the composition of affective relations between individuals, together with the 'plane of consistency' on which they interact, that is, their environment." This environment is "a field of forces" and "the ground on which the unconscious is constructed" (Hurley 1988, ii). Pleasant interactions could occur in the classroom which could prepare citizens to live in the "good" or border city. The "unit of understanding" would not be the "at-risk" child or the parent who did not care about education but rather the efforts of the teacher in creating "the composition of affective relations." Success for the teacher would be the creation of an environment in which many organized encounters could occur. This measurement of success is not unlike Freire's definition of success when he argues that the classroom as an effective learning environment rather than the individual student should be our focus in assessment. The creation of an environment in which many organized encounters could occur could be accomplished through curricular changes and a reconfiguration of the teacher-student relationship leading towards experiential learning. The teacher could understand that education is an interactive process, not a passive one.

Third, in a multicultural, Spinozian "good" classroom, the teacher would make the effort to organize pleasant encounters across cultural, ethnic, gender, and other differences. Students would be taught to perceive and comprehend that which they have in common even with those they find to be disagreeable. A concrete example of this can be taken from the situation of the high-functioning autistic child in the classroom. The teacher needs to prevent other students from teasing or bullying the child while at the same time helping the child to learn to develop the skills of social interaction.

What opportunities for organized encounter could occur in the multicultural classroom, as opposed to the "good" or border city? Exposure to cultural, ethnic, religious, and gender diversity makes it possible to be affected in a great number of ways, which may increase the power of the subject. Such exposure can occur in the border city. The city, however, is most often segregated ethnically and economically. As an environment, change can be effected more easily within the class than within an entire city. There is one problem, however, that must be considered. The student population in a city such as San Diego is much more diverse than the teacher population. In some parts of the district, there are over 400 minority students per minority teacher. Students need role models who resemble them physically and culturally, and student-teacher and teacher-parent interactions will be made easier when African-American students have African-American teachers, for example. (DeVise 1997, A1, A14). This is not to say that a student can only learn from someone of the same ethnic background, of course, but in a school district such as San Diego's there is a serious imbalance. Nevertheless, teachers and students can organize their encounters with greater ease than in the city. With important exceptions, the classroom, not including the playground, the parking lot, the halls and the grounds, is physically safer than the city and is more conducive to organized encounters than is the city.

Fourth, what example of the common notion could we imagine in a classroom situation? According to Deleuze, "the first common notions are . . . the least general ones" (1988, 56). These represent something in common between me and another "that affects me with joy-passion" (56). In other words, if I already find someone pleasant, charming, easier to get along with, similar to me or non threatening, the common notion, or that category that will express what is common between me and that person can be quite specific. The other person and I have a certain luxury in this case. In fact, I may feel joy-passion when I encounter "a body" or person that agrees with me even without knowing what "it" has in common with me. The affect, or emotion, of joy, an active passion, follows from the common notion; conversely, on occasion, the common notion can follow from joy (56–57). The common notion is not a passion itself, but it leads to a passion. The situation becomes more complex when I interact with someone I find to be unpleasant, rude, difficult to get along with, threatening, repulsive, loathsome, less than human, weak, despicable, and so on. Depending on my referential codes, the person could be revolting to me for religious, class, ethnic, or other reasons. Whatever my reasons, a chance interaction with this person is likely to be unpleasant. The solution offered by Spinoza for this social problem is that of the common notion. Somehow, a category, concept, or idea must be found that can express what is common between us. Where do we get the strength, desire or "force" to seek such a notion? (56) We get this strength from the first common notions, which, we remember, occur when we come into contact with those whom we find to be agreeable (agradable). Those common notions lead to joy, and that joy is the "force" which helps us to form more general common notions which we will need with people we find disagreeable. Obviously, we need some way to guide ourselves to joyful interactions or our "force" will become depleted. We can now discuss Spinoza's concept of reason. Reason is first, the "effort to select and organize good encounters," and second, the ability to perceive and comprehend common notions (56–57).

The third part of this journey, which will consist of five brief forays, is an exploration of strategies for the radical restructuring of society. As I mentioned earlier in this chapter, Foucault's work can lead us to a vision of such restructuring. I now want to examine the passage about "subjects of power" in detail and in relation to theories of social change mentioned in this book and to Spinoza. How might the radical restructuring of society that Darder finds to be a necessary part of critical pedagogy take place? We can begin with five ways taken from Foucault.

First, we must begin with what Foucault calls an historical ontology of ourselves. In the U.S.-Mexico border region, how border subjects have been produced, in an historical sense, can be addressed. In the multicultural classroom, this discussion can be extended to include all represented subjects. For example, what is whiteness? How has the category changed historically? When did "gay" become a category?

Does "gay" have the same meaning internationally? Is a young Mexican man with a wife and a child who makes his living as a male prostitute in Tijuana "in the closet" or making a living? What is the historical ontology of the immigrant? How do these questions relate to Spinozian reason? Is the undocumented maid who works in La Jolla able to organize pleasant encounters with thieves on the trolley she rides home at night to Tijuana? Is the immigrant just learning English able to perceive and comprehend common notions? Can Koreans do this as shop owners with African-American customers in Los Angeles? Can Latinos and African-Americans do this as high school students? Do wealthy whites in gated communities have the experience of joy-passion that gives them the "force" to find common notions in their encounters with the homeless and the Other?

Second, what is the genealogy of the constitution of our social being? In a fully constituted state, subjects would be "autonomous producers of wealth, knowledge, and cooperation, without the need of external command, when they organize production and social reproduction" (Hardt and Negri 1994, 311). In a multicultural classroom, the student can work backward from this definition to the way in which s/he or his/her family or community has been restricted from producing or forced to produce wealth for others. Students can examine what definitions of knowledge existed in their cultures of origin and how those definitions differ from those in the culture in which they currently live. The mechanisms by which those groups most criminalized in this culture, African-American and Latino males, are reproduced can be analyzed. The perceived need for external command, in gender relations, the workplace, vestiges of feudal relations that continue to characterize class relations, and misplaced patriotism and allegiance in relation to an oppressive state can be revealed for what they share: resentment against life that links the oppressor and the oppressed. By understanding how they have participated in destroying the construction of the conditions of freedom, and without proposing a utopian model, students can see how they might participate in constructing the conditions of freedom. This is different from offering students a utopian model. Analysis of the genealogy of the constitution of our social being as multicultural selves can lead the student to a glimpse of the genealogy of the new subject: autonomous, productive, democratic, choosing freedom over oppression, life-affirming.

Third, how are we constructed as subjects of knowledge? From a Spinozian perspective, our interaction with things and our understanding of things cannot be separated. Our ability to organize our interactions with things shapes our construction as subjects of knowledge. Related to this question is what Foucault calls "the knowledge that can be gained of us" (Foucault 1979, 294). Darder argues that in order to understand the relationship between culture and power, we must also attend to the relationship between "what is considered truth (knowledge) and power." Darder explains that in the multicultural classroom, "the ability of individuals from different cultural groups to express their cultural truths is clearly related to the power that certain groups are able to wield in the social order." She concludes that "any educational theory of cultural democracy" must examine how this knowledge is reproduced in educational institutions and in the society as a whole (1991, 27–28).

Fourth, how are we constructed as subjects of power? Foucault emphasizes the productive and not just the negative aspects of power:

> In fact, power produces. It produces reality; it produces domains of objects and rituals of truth. The individual and the knowledge that can be gained of him belong to this production.' (1979, 194).

In what Foucault calls the carceral society, individuals are controlled and produced by "large, invisible structures of official power" (quoted in Booker 1996, 126). Although it may appear that Foucault returns to the very definition of power he rejects, repression, it is his emphasis on the productive aspect of power that is significant here. By redefining power as productive and not just repressive, Foucault prepares the ground for understanding Spinoza's definition of power, which will eventually lead us to an understanding of how to free ourselves from the large, invisible structures of official power.

In Deleuze's explanation of Spinoza's definition of power, "all power is inseparable from a capacity of being affected" (1998, 97). Deleuze distinguishes between two kinds of power: (1) immobilized, reactive power and (2) expansive power. In the first, we want to destroy the object that is the cause of our sad affects; in the second, we want to unite with the object that is the cause of our joy-affect. Deleuze writes, referring to Part IV, "Of Human Bondage, or the Nature of the Emotions," Proposition 18 of Spinoza's *Ethics*:

> in sadness our power as a *conatus* serves entirely to invest the painful trace and to repel or destroy the object which is its cause. Our power is immobilized, and can no longer do anything but react. In joy on the contrary, our

power expands compounds with the power of the other, and unites with the loved object (Deleuze 1988, 101).

He defines *conatus* as the "effort to persevere in existing and to act under the guidance of Reason" (103). By first understanding that we are produced, and not repressed by power, we can focus on how to transform our immobilized, reactive power into expansive power.

Fifth, how are we constructed as moral subjects of action? Deleuze distinguishes between the terms moral and ethical. He claims that Spinoza's ethics is a theory of power while morality is a theory of obligations (1988, 104). From a Spinozian perspective, we cannot be active, ethical individuals if we are mired in sad, passive affects. If we understand morality as a system of good and evil, then Foucault is asking us to see how we are labeled within, produced by, reproduced by, and trapped by this system. This is the definition of morality that Nietzsche attacks in *Beyond Good and Evil*. Without the ability to be reasonable, in Spinoza's sense of being able to perceive and comprehend common notions, we cannot be ethical; to be ethical and able to act demands the ability to transform sad, passive affects into joy-passions.

The fourth stop on this journey is an analysis of the ethical components of the "good" classroom as it relates to the state. As Giroux and McLaren write in their essay "Writing from the Margins"

> radical educational theorists as a group have eschewed trying to develop a theory of ethics that can either justify our own language or legitimate the social practices necessary for defending a particular vision of what schools might become (1997, 19).

They claim, rightly, that there has been an inability to move from a posture of criticism to one of vision due to the paradoxical cage in which radical educational theorists have been trapped, that of moral indignation without a theory of ethics (1997, 19). The discussion of ethics is linked to democracy. As McLaren explains in an interview with Gert Biesta and Siebren Miedema, the term "democracy" is highly suspect in Latin America, in his words, "a smokescreen for exploitation for creating a dependency economy" (McLaren 1997, 232). Therefore, I begin this endeavor by recognizing both the need for a theory of ethics and McLaren's cautionary note concerning the term "democracy."

How can we proceed from dialectical thought to the model of a democratic state that I am putting forward? Adorno is useful in his emphasis on nonidentity. The general concept of nonidentity which undermines the notion of the norm, can be used to heighten our sensitivity to individual differences in the classroom. That is, if nothing can be precisely equal to anything else, then the notion of a norm loses its power. Let us imagine a Chicana sixth grader struggling with gender issues. She is impatient with and sometimes hostile towards boys, who find her attractive In an identity-driven classroom in which heterosexuality is compulsory, chance encounters between this girl and male students will most likely be unpleasant. The same boys who find her attractive might be shocked to find out she is attracted to girls. They might tease her. If gender studies can be made part of the curriculum, the environment changes. I am not calling here merely for a shift in consciousness, but in unconsciousness. Furthermore, it is not only a mental shift. Gay-bashing demands a response that rejects the mind-body split.

This example draws on Adorno's concept of nonidentity. It also creates a space for critical pedagogy and dialectical thought or the seeking out of social contradictions in the gender studies curriculum. At this point in the example, some kind of conflict resolution is indicated. Spinoza's concept of consciousness has been mentioned; I now want to refer to his concepts of adequate ideas and joyful passions, which are his solution to the problem of conflict. The adequate idea comes from the common notion, which has to do with finding something in common with someone, even someone whom we find disagreeable. If we define the self as unified, centered, and bound, it is hard to imagine how this might occur. However, as Deleuze reads Spinoza, we are individuals existing in an environment or field of forces. In his preface to Deleuze's *Spinoza*, Robert Hurley writes:

> Deleuze opens us to the idea (which I take as a contribution to ecological thought) that the elements of the different individuals we compose may be nonhuman *within* us. What we are capable of may partake of the wolf, the river, the stone in the river. One wonders, finally, whether man is anything more than a territory, a set of boundaries, a limit on existence (1988, iii).

The final sentence in this passage is a critique of the arbitrary, common-sense definition of the individual as a separate, delineated personality and a body ending at our skin. In this poetic, expansive definition of the individual, the possibilities of finding something in common with another individual are much broader than class, race, gender, national origin, or religion. They are even broader than shared political viewpoint or common interests. We get glimpses into a world informed by this view in the works of Carlos Castaneda, R. Anaya's *Bless Me Última*, and certain episodes of *Star Trek*. Just as we are redefining citizenship to go beyond national boundaries and to depend on meaningful participation in communities that do not respect national boundaries, so in this definition we are redefining the individual to go beyond the traditional view of the consistent, centered, bounded self and to depend on commonality and joyful interaction with other individuals who do not respect the Western, Oedipal, capitalist boundaries of subjected selves. In short, the boundaries of ourselves can be redrawn or ignored by us.

In a more mundane sense, we can return to our example. In this classroom of sixth-graders, there is also a boy experiencing a gender crisis similar to the girl's. In their interaction, the common notion could be quite specific, such as a shared interest in art. An extremely homophobic boy in the class and the girl in our example would need a much more general notion to express their commonality. A pronouncement by the teacher in a lecture-style traditional classroom to the effect of "You're both human, now try to get along," would be ineffective. Only an organized encounter in an environment such as the "good" classroom could create the conditions for a pleasant interaction.

I have experienced a situation similar to the one I am describing. In a class in which I taught Anzaldúa's *Borderlands*, several Latinos were contemptuous of the book and disruptive during classroom discussions. They had no interest in discussing gender issues and asked various female classmates, rudely, if they were lesbians. One of the students, to whom I referred earlier in this book, used his background as a priest and a healer to establish commonality at many levels. First, he was able to gain trust as an ex-Catholic, because they were Catholic. Second, as a Latino male, even though he was gay, they felt more comfortable with him than they did with Anglo feminists. Third, as a healer and as someone who had grown up in a neighborhood similar to theirs, he was able to get them to discuss the repressed pain and sadness they had with regard to friends of theirs who had been killed in gang-related violence. This was done in a small group. The shared referential codes kept creating a larger territory of commonality until finally, the anger these students had expressed in their chance encounter with Anzaldúa's book was transformed into first sadness and later community and solidarity. At the end of the class, they were participating in class discussions. Their fear of homosexuality was no longer an issue; their concern was explaining to the class the culture in which they had been unable to mourn for the friends they had lost. On the last day of class, when the student-healer built an altar, they participated in the ritual, and the process of passive, sad affects being transformed into active, joyful affects was complete.

For such environments to become more widespread, there must be a radical restructuring of society in which gays, lesbians, and bisexuals are participants in a fully constituted state. In the meantime, to return to the example of the gender-confused sixth grader, conflict resolution is a better response than platitudes. At the very least, the referential codes of students can be increased through an expansion of the curriculum to include gender studies. In this way, the three elements of Spinoza's *Ethics*—adequate ideas, consciousness, and joyful passions—can become part of the "good" multicultural classroom. A maximization of joyful passions can take place through sociality; adequate ideas can be formed through the common notion and by "denouncing all that separates us from life" (Deleuze 1988, 26), including sad passions. One can become conscious of oneself through interaction with others, inside and outside the classroom.

In the fifth and final part of this journey, I want to attend to the implications of bicultural pedagogy for border theory and vice versa. I want to clarify for the reader the relationship between the border subject, biculturalism, a stereoscopic or holographic view, doubled referential codes, and the common notion. All forms of biculturalism create the possibility for a greater number of common notions. Braidotti's emphasis on the transnational labor force can be linked to border pedagogy, because increased immigration results in a need for border pedagogy. It is in the border city that there is both the greatest potential and the greatest danger for conflict resolution and the joyful, organized encounter. Bicultural pedagogy is a call for protecting the bicultural environment inside and outside of the classroom.

Closely related to this discussion of the ethical border subject is McLaren's discussion of the struggle for the ethical self in relation to postmodern culture, revolutionary multiculturalism and critical pedagogy. In the introduction to this chapter, I referred to Hardt and Negri's notion of "affective labor." McLaren calls on us to follow Paul Trembath

in utilizing Deleuze's work on "affective capacities" in conjunction with a revised Marxian theory of sensuous activity in ways that are compatible with poststructuralist theories of difference and cultural materalism's opposition to the idealization of sense. In other words, we need a new language and politics of the body (McLaren 1995).

Using Trembath's concept (1996), I am claiming that these "affective capacities" are increased in the border dweller, who is able to be affected in a greater number of ways.

Trembath clearly explains how Derrida and Foucault's critique of the subject, and specifically, humanist agency, does not include an alternative notion of agency: "neither of them manage to situate active power convincingly once they've done away with humanism" (Trembath 1996,141). He notes that Deleuze, on the other hand, "associates the action of bodies with relational affects, never simply with autonomous subjects or human deliberators" (Trembath, 142). Trembath's discussion of "sensuous accumulation" and Hardt and Negri's notion of "affective labor" overlap in the very important area of suggesting a new theory of value. Just as the value of the labor of the health worker or the AIDS activist cannot be understood without attention to the affective aspect of their labor, so is there a "sense-devaluation" in relation to cultural capital:

> No one associates creativity with anything but our capitalized sense of art-istry (or by now famous criticism); no one will become activist unless they sense a surplus of attention that tells them that they can (that they *should*); no one recognizes their own powers of sensuous accumulation as the already active producers of capital (after all, who publicizes or values *that*, so why should we?). Finally, no one understands their affective capacities as forever active *creative power* (Trembath 1996, 144).

We should avoid creating a dichotomy between what appears to be a difference, that Hardt and Negri on focus on labor while Trembath directs his attention to art or culture. As Trembath reminds us, in the context of the early Marx, such a distinction is unnecessary: "It is well known that the early Marx emphasized the importance of concepts such as "sensuous practice," "labor," and "use value" as both critical and experiential alternative to the corruptions of "capital," "exchange value," and so forth" (Trembath 1996, 135).

At the beginning of this study, which has attempted to explore the relationships between a theory of labor, a theory of the state, and the issues of gender and culture/"race"/ethnicity, there was a crucial missing link. It appeared in the disjuncture between feminism and Marxism, as various theories were considered. While the issue of racism was addressed in Gutiérrez-Jones's work in relation to the state, the dilemma of the unhappy marriage between Marxism and feminism remained. In the work of Hardt and Negri, a significant juxtaposition was made between an affective theory of labor and the notion of the cyborg. Drawing on the work of feminist critics who have redefined what should be considered of value and as labor, Hardt and Negri broadened their concept of labor. Negri's previous work laid the groundwork for the inclusion of this feminist contribution insofar as he had already attacked labor, in its use by both Marxists and capitalists, as a bourgeois concept.

Proceeding from an affective theory of labor, which suggests a new theory of value, we can reconceptualize citizenship, community, work, and pedagogy. In Spinoza's ethics, sad affects lead to passivity, and joyful, active affects to action. Through the common notion, and joyful encounters in the "good" City, including joyful encounters in the context of work, passivity can be transformed into activity. The "good" City can also be the imagined community or the multicultural classroom. In the Chicana lesbian, the two examples of affective labor are brought together, feminism and activism. Following Hardt and Negri, we see that the immaterial, technological (scientific), affective and co-operative aspects of labor must be recognized. In this context, "the production of subjectivity is always a process of hybridization, border crossing, and in contemporary history this subjective hybrid is produced increasingly at the interface between the human and the machine" (1994, 13–14). This subject is being produced at the U.S.-Mexican border in the border machine, in robo-raza, the woman *maquila* worker, in the cyber-educator of the multicultural future, and in the *barrio* mother who picks her daughter up from the computer club. She may refuse to recognize national boundaries as she continues to build communities across them with or without citizenship; the very presence of her voice, which will not be silenced, offers the possibility of disruptive rhetorical options.

Note

1. See Derek Heater (1990). For a discussion of migrant communities, see Roger Rouse (1989).

Conclusion

Beyond the Classroom, Beyond the Nation

This book is about the multiplicities of cultures and intelligences in the classroom as it will exist in the next century in the United States. Rather than following the British colonial model, which was to teach those in the colonies about geraniums (Viswanathan 1989), I have put forward the view that the multicultural classroom can become a place in which Foucault's dictum may take place, by asking how we are constructed as subjects of knowledge, constituted as subjects of power, and constituted as moral subjects of action; that is, it is here that the student may explore how he or she is becoming a subject. In the Introduction, "Critical Pedagogies and Literacies in the Borderlands," I discuss an overview of the book. The basic approach, pedagogical theory from Freire to Darder (1991), is laid out. I conclude that since both Deleuzians and critics writing about pedagogical theory claim Foucault, it is possible that pedagogical theory can be grounded in the Deleuzian tradition rather than merely orthodox marxism or Frankfurt theory. This entails a search for a clearer definition of critical theory in Darder and in exploring critiques of Jameson (1986), a marxist critic who has written about the revision of the canon, such as Aijad Ahmad's (1987). Ahmad's critique of Jameson includes the observation that he does not pay significant attention to issues of gender. In an attempt to focus on gender as well as multiculturalism, pedagogical issues, and the relationship between the classroom and the state, I make the Chicana central in this study.

A feminist critic who has already made links between Deleuze (1986) and feminist theory is Rosi Braidotti (1994).[1] In addition, she emphasizes the importance of beginning feminist inquiry from an understanding of one's own location. The present study has begun from the location of the U.S.-Mexico border. The Chicana's positioning on a variety of borders, particularly her relationship to capitalism, as a member of the most stable part of the transnational working class, make her a relevant figure of study in the conceptualization of these issues. In chapter 1, "Nationalism, History, the Chicano/a Subject, and the Text," I discuss the need for attention to the Dionysian in Chicano culture, the voice of the Chicana, and more specifically, the Chicana lesbian. I mention Nietzsche in this chapter in part in order to prepare for the reader for a non-Hegelian thread that would link Nietzsche and Deleuze. In chapter 2, "Boundaries in the Classroom: Teacher-Student 'Contact Zones' and Spinoza's Good Classroom," I discuss Spinoza's "good" City (1992) in relation to the multicultural classroom. In response to the argument that contractual theories do not make a place for women, I argue, in chapter 6, that Spinoza's theory, as articulated by Hardt and Negri (1994) and linked to the notion of affective labor, creates a space for a response to Pateman's (1988) critique. That is, in Spinoza's theory of affects, as it can be related to affective labor, there is the possibility of reconceptualizing gender in relation to work. Spinoza is not used arbitrarily, but because of his importance in the work of Negri. Negri's work is what I am offering as an alternative, or at least a complement, to the Freirian theorists who look to Marxism and the Frankfurt School as the basis of critical pedagogy. I also refer to the work of Macedo (1994, 1996), who interviews Freire about issues he did not address in earlier work, including gender issues. In both the work of Freire and that of Hardt and Negri, there is the call for what the latter describe as "a continuous, metaphysical construction of the conditions of freedom" (1994, 312). Underlying the conditions of freedom is rhetorical freedom. In chapter 5, "Culture, Narrativity and Assessment," I identify areas in which pedagogical theorists might more carefully delineate what they mean by critical theory.

In chapter 3, "Literacy and the Teaching of Literature for Bilingual and Bicultural Students," I argue that there is a need for multiple literacies and examine the significance of hybrid spaces. It is in hybrid spaces that the Dionysian desire can escape. An analogous "escape" is occurring internationally in the situation of the woman migrant. Her existence and the way in which she is neither legal nor illegal, throw into question the notion of the nation and suggest that it is outdated, according to Adelaida Del Castillo.[2] Furthermore, as Aronowitz and Di Fazio argue (1994), there is a massive displacement of workers at all levels, despite claims that there is a move towards a knowledge-based, high-tech workplace. They advocate the reduction of the workday without a reduction of pay. Just as the woman migrant work throws the nation as a concept into question, so pay without work calls into question the notion of value in a capitalist society. If an education does not guarantee a job, and in the future, we may not even work full-time, then how might we reconceptualize both school and the workplace?

In chapters 4 and 6, "The Marketing of Ethnic Studies, Attacks on Affirmative Action, and the Obfuscation of 'Whiteness'" and "Immigration, Emigration, and Literary Analysis: Voices of the Not-Quite-White," I interrogate the term "white." Again, it is the hybrid space, in this case, the person of mixed race, which throws into question the black/white opposition. In these chapters, I argue that an interrogation of whiteness is essential to understanding its power in the classroom.

In chapter 7, "Pedagogical Implications of the Deleuzo-Guattarian Perspective: from Negri to Darder," I look at theories of the state, new definitions of citizenship, theories of labor and value, and the concept of critical thinking. I object to Giroux's (1991) use of Adorno in that he does not clarify the relationship between the Frankfurt School and Marxism; the importance of nonidentity in Adorno's negative dialectic is not stressed. Nonidentity is an important aspect of the postmodern, and forms part of the cultural capital of Latino culture. I find Darder's definition of power to be problematic. I refer to the difficulties raised by a notion of a political consciousness and the charge that has been brought against Friere, that his theory is Leninist. It is Aronowitz's defense of Freire, in which they argue that Freire calls on workers to share their power over knowledge, that reverses the hierarchy of the avant-garde intellectual over the worker and brings Freire closer to Foucault and Negri and Hardt.

Despite the inconsistencies in argumentation in the pedagogical theorists considered here, their call for a radical pedagogy, following Freire, must be heeded. As Darder makes explicit, and as is blatantly clear in the borderlands, reform in the classroom will only be undermined if it is not accompanied by radical change outside the classroom. The problem, however, is that marxism has not been sympathetic to minorities, so further work must be done in order to take Darder's call for radical social change seriously.

Negri is useful in considering the relationship between the classroom and the state. What is the relationship between Negri's state and the postnational era in which we live? Negri's essays considered here do not address gender or race specifically; however, in the sections written with Hardt, through the notion of affective labor, a conceptual space is created for these concerns.[3] The category of affective labor, considered in conjunction with Haraway's cyborg (1991) and Del Castillo's reconsideration of citizenship, point the way towards the development of a theoretical basis for the development of a truly radical project of critical pedagogy. This project would not merely address the needs of monocultural students, or of middle-class or gifted child, nor would it be a ghetto for all other children. Rather, in a Freirian sense, it would allow for children of all backgrounds and social classes to express themselves, and it would draw on the cultural capital of surrounding communities in order to do so.

In the introduction, I mentioned West's (1982) definition of the age that is about to end, an age which he argues began with the expulsion of the Jew in Spain. I pointed out that intentionally, or not, West placed the Jew in an interesting position, as he or she who could not be assimilated, neither in 1492 in Spain nor in 1945 in Germany. Even today, the Jew is not quite white. I am bringing the work of Spinoza, a philosopher who was a Jew condemned as a heretic in his own community, back into the Latino community, but this time, not to Spain, but to the U.S.-Mexico border.

It is Spinoza's model of the "good" City that I have extended to the "good" classroom. In the normal city, we find urban dwellers who do not all perceive the world the same way, and whose chance interactions are often unpleasant, whereas in the "good" City, through the "common notion," city dwellers can function together in a microcosm of an alternative form of democracy. I have argued that it is in the classroom that we can see Spinoza's "good" City, or Negri's state fully constituted by the multitude. A model of this city can be the border city.

Now, in more practical terms, I want to discuss the work of Del Castillo, who argues (as does Meehan) that there is a new kind of citizenship emerging. Specifically, it is the Mexican immigrant woman who forms this community in the border region. Del Castillo states that like the multinational corporations, these migrant women do not respect national boundaries. They may not have "citizenship" according to U.S. law, but under an expanded, postnational definition of the term, they are citizens. That is, their community-building is redefining citizenship. In the US.-Mexico border region, they are part of the community Darder describes as a necessary part of a radical pedagogy.

I want to refer to the Purépecha definition of nation, which conjoins people, land and work.[4] This definition is interesting when read in relation to (1) Del Castillo's thesis and (2) the work of Aronowitz and DiFazio. Migrant woman who return to Aztlan to work may fit into the Purepecha definition, especially in the case of those communities described by Roger Rouse (1989). In relation to Aronowitz and DiFazio, the definition is significant because it suggests that if one part of the tripartite definition changes, then changes in the other parts would be implied. Aronowitz and de Fazio argue that the definition of work is being changed as the work week is shortened. If work is no longer to be conceived of in the same way, and if nation-states are becoming obsolete, and if the situation of the deterritorialized or border subject is becoming the norm, then we can speak of life as no longer defined by work as labor, of the citizen/subject as no longer limited to one nation, and of a community no longer confined by national boundaries.

How will the city be defined in this scenario? The city will no longer be defined by work as labor and industry as alienating technology, its citizens will no longer be limited to one nation, and its communities will not be defined by national boundaries. Cities that are harbingers of these changes are border cities, in which families exist on both sides of an international border, in which more than one currency is used, in which more than one language plays a major role in the everyday life of citizens, and in which the term *citizen* is itself being debated. This city will be a virtual city, on-line, with e-mail being the way its citizens communicate.

To create the conditions for pleasant encounters in the border city can be seen as a task of the multicultural classroom. However, just as the border city offers the possibilities being discussed, it is also a place in which fear is instilled, differences emphasized in order to create conflict. The punishment of undocumented immigrants serves to discipline documented immigrants. The model of democracy I am putting forward here is not the one taught to children in schools in the United States. As Cornel West (1982) reminds us, American democracy is based on the enslavement of Africans, over 20 percent of the population of the nation at the time. Spinoza gives only the category of the common notion as a way to imagine how the citizens of the "good" City might have pleasant encounters. To this I would like to recall other models that have been discussed throughout this book. Kristeva's (1986) semiotic or *chora* is the border imaginary, which remains the Deleuzo-Guattarian language of the dream, which, in their discussion of Kafka, they identify as Hebrew.[5] Dwellers in the border-lands, however, have different languages of the dream; for some, it is Spanish, for some, it is Portuguese or Italian or Tagalog; for others, such as the Native Americans living on reservations, it is the indig-enous language being lost, which was replaced by Spanish, and is now being replaced by English.

As Negri and Hardt argue, the multitude must have power over knowledge and wealth. In the borderlands, the immigrant and the bor-der dweller who has had the border redrawn around him or her share a common fate; to be directly and strategically involved in a struggle for this power over knowledge and wealth It is Dionysian desire that propels us out of our norms, rules, definitions, communities, along with political upheavals, and it is this same desire that forms new communities aboard, about, above, across, after, against, along, amid, among, around and at the edges of language, alterity, and difference.

Notes

1. I am particularly receptive, on a personal level, to Braidotti's work because she is an Italian working in Utrecht, that is, a woman of the South living and working in the North. My own background is Italian, German and English. I have spent most of my life in the U.S.-Mexico border region. My grandfather, who was of Sicilian descent, insisted that the grandchildren learn Spanish since he found Mexican culture to be more similar to Italian culture. Although I live and work in the Chicano community, and my son is bilingual and bicultural, I am both an insider and an outsider. At the time of the writing of *Border Writing*, I was unable to clearly articulate the relationship between Chicano culture, which is of course rooted in the culture of the U.S.-Mexico border, and border culture as a model which is postnational. Since that time, there is a very clear situation in which historical events are forcing a clearer articulation of this dilemma. The Chicano movement itself is struggling with the question of whether or not Salvadorans are Chicano. In my view, Chicano culture has put forward a model of border culture. Personally, it was the model of border culture with which I was most familiar. The way that I am using border culture in the present work, however, is not to be simplistically equated with Chicano culture. Rosi Braidotti sets forth her views on Deleuze, including her reservations about some of his work, in *Nomadic Subjects*. For an excellent study of Deleuze and feminist readers of Deleuze, including Braidotti, see Elizabeth Grosz (1994).

2. Adelaida Del Castillo March, personal conversations with author, March 1997.

3. Michael Hardt, e-mail to the author, 25 April 1997.

4. Phone conversation with Alurista, 22 March 1997. After discussing Adelaida Del Castillo's conference paper with Alurista, he told me about a conversation he had had a few months ago with Juan Gómez-Quiñones and Adelaida Del Castillo. Different positions were taken on the definition of the nation. Alurista recounted that he had put forward the Purépecha concept of nation as people, land and work.

5. See Kristeva (1986, 94–96), on dream logic and semiotic memory. See also Deleuze and Guattari (1986).

Bibliography

Acuna, Rodolfo. 1996. *Anything But Mexican, Chicanas in Contemporary Los Angeles*. London and New York: Verso.

Adorno, Theodor. 1991. *Notes on Literature*. Ed. Rolf Tiedemann. Trans. Shierry Weber Nicholsen. New York: Columbia University Press.

―――. 1973. *Negative Dialectics*. Trans. E. B. Ashton. New York: Seabury.

―――. 1983. *Prisms*. London: Neville Spearman.

―――. 1976. "Sociology and Empirical Research." In *The Positivist Dispute in German Sociology*, ed. Theodor W. Adorno *et. al.*, trans. Glyn Adey and David Frisby. London: Heineman.

Ahmad, Aijad. 1987. "Jameson's Rhetoric of Otherness and the 'Allegory.'" *Social Text* 17 (Fall): 3–25.

Ahponen, Pirkkoliisa. 1997. Letter to author. 21 March.

Alurista. 1997. Telephone conversation with author. 22 March.

―――. 1993. 1 June. Lecture. Department of Literature. University of California, San Diego.

Anzaldúa, Gloria. 1993. *Friends from the Other Side. Amigos del otro lado*. San Francisco: Children's Book Press.

―――. 1987. *Borderlands, La Frontera*. San Francisco: spinster/ aunt lute.

Arguelles, Lourdes. 1990. "Undocumented Female Labor in the United States Southwest: An Essay on Migration, Consciousness, Oppression and Struggle." In *Between Borders: Essays on*

Mexicana/Chicana History, ed. Adelaida R. Del Castillo. Encino, CA: Floricanto Press. 299–312.

Aronowitz, Stanley. 1996. Interview by Shirley Steinberg. *Measured Lies, The Bell Curve Examined*, ed. J. Kincheloe, Shirley R. Steinberg, and Aaron D. Gresson III. New York: St. Martin's Press. 137–60.

————. 1994. *Dead Artists, Live Theories and Other Cultural Problems*. New York: Routledge.

Aronowitz, Stanley, and William Di Fazio. 1994. *The Jobless Future, Sci-Tech and the Dogma of Work*. Minneapolis and London: University of Minnesota Press.

Aronowitz, Stanley, and Henry Giroux. 1994. *Education Still under Siege*. Critical Studies in Education and Culture Series. Westport, Conn.: Bergin and Garvey.

Beck, R. 1991. *General Education: Vocational and Academic Collaboration*. Berkeley, CA, NCRVE.

Bejar, Ruth. 1993. *Translated Woman, Crossing the Border with Esperanza's Story*. Boston: Beacon.

Benhabib, Seyla. 1992. The Utopian Dimension in Communicative Ethics. In *Situating the Self, Gender, Community and Postmodernism in Contemporary Ethics*. New York: Routledge. n.p. .

Benjamin, Walter. 1969. *Illuminations*. New York: Schocken.

Berlin, James A. 1993. "Literacy, Pedagogy, and English Studies: Postmodern Connections." In *Critical Literacy, Politics, Praxis and the Postmodern*, ed. Colin Lankshear and Peter L. McLaren. Teacher Empowerment and School Reform Series. Albany: SUNY Press. 247–267. Quoting Robert Scholes. 1985. *Textual Power: Literary Theory and the Teaching of English*. New Haven: Yale University Press

Bhabha, Homi K 1984. "Of Mimicry and Man: the Ambivalence of Colonial Discourse." *October* 28: 128–33.

Bloch, Ernst. 1977. "Nonsynchrony and Its Obligation to Dialectics." *New German Critique* 4 no. 2:22–38.

Booker, M. Keith. 1996. *A Practical Introduction to Literary Theory and Criticism.* White Plains, N. Y.: Longman. Quoting Salman Rushdie. 1982. "The Empire Writes Back with a Vengeance." *London Times.* 3 July. 8.

Bové, Paul. 1992. "The Intellectual as a Contemporary Phenomenon." In *Rethinking Culture Conference Proceedings, University of Montreal, Montreal, 3–5 April.* Online. Altavista. Internet. 3 Jan. 1997. Http://elias.ens.fr/Surfaces/vol2/bove.html.

Braidotti, Rosi. 1995. "Turn the Challenge of Europe to Our Feminist Advantage." "Women and Internationalization." Public meeting arranged by KVINFO. 28 November. Online. Altavista. Internet. 9 July 1997. Http://www.kulturnt.dk/homes/ kvinfo/ fordele.thml.

————. *Nomadic Subjects: Patterns of Dissonance.* Embodiment and Difference in Contemporary Theory Series. New York: Columbia University Press, 1994.

Braun, Gerry, and Ruth L. McKinnie. 1997. "San Diego Race Relations End with a Few Sour Notes." *San Diego Union* 12 June. n.p.

Buchanan, Ruth. 1995. "Border Crossings, NAFTA, Regulatory Restructuring and the Politics of Place." *Global Legal Studies Journal* 2.2 (Spring) 1–18. Online. Altavista. Internet. 8 July 1997. Http://www.law.indiana.edu/glsj/vol2/no2/buchanan.html.

Burgos-Debray, Elisabeth. 1984. *I, Rigoberta Menchú; An Indian Woman in Guatemala.* London: Verso.

Cary, Richard. 1996. "IQ a Commodity: The 'New' Economics of Intelligence." In *Measured Lies: The Bell Curve Examined,* ed. Joe L. Kincheloe, Shirley R. Steinberg, and Aaron R. Gresson III. New York: St. Martin's. 137–60.

Castillo, Ana. 1995. *Massacre of the Dreamers: Essays on Xicanisma.* New York: Penguin/Dutton/Signet.

Cervantes, Alma E. 1996. "Had I Ironed Your Shirt?" 2nd ed. In *Chicana Creativity and Criticism: New Frontiers in American Literature,* ed. Maria Herrera-Sobek, and Helena María Viramontes. University of New Mexico.

Cisneros, Sandra. 1994. *The House on Mango Street.* New York: Knopf.

―――. "Red Clowns." 1994. *The House on Mango Street.* New York: Knopf.

―――. "Hair." 1994. *The House on Mango Street.* New York: Knopf.

Collins, Marie and Sue Anderson. 14 June. 1993. "Affirmation, Resistance, Transformation." ACLS Curriculum Project. UCLA. Rancho Mirage, CA.

――― 1992–1995. Team Based Curriculum: The Emergence of the Chicano. ACLS Curriculum Project. UCLA.

Collins, James. 1993. "Determination and Contradiction: An Appreciation and Critique of the Work of Pierre Bourdieu in Language and Education." In *Bourdieu: Critical Perspectives,* ed. Craig Calhoun, Edward LiPuma, and Moishe Postone. Chicago: University of Chicago Press. n.p. Quoting Pierre Bourdieu and Jean-Claude Passeron. 1997. *Reproduction in Education, Society and Culture.* London: Sage.

Cortázar, Julio. 1973. *Libro de Manuel.* Buenos Aires: Sudamericana.

―――. 1963. *Rayuela.* Buenos Aires: Sudamericana.

Darder, Antonia. 1991. *Culture and Power in the Classroom: A Critical Foundation for Bicultural Education.* Westport: Bergin and Garvey. Quoting Henry Giroux. *Theory and Resistance in Education.* New York: Bergin. 1983. n.p.

Del Castillo, Adelaida. 1997. Conversations with author. March.

―――. Introduction: Trouble and Ethnographic Endeavor. Unpublished. n.d.

Deleuze, Gilles. 1992. *Expressionism in Philosophy: Spinoza.* Trans. Martin Joughin. New York: Zone.

―――. 1988. *Spinoza: Practical Philosophy.* Trans. Robert Hurley. San Francisco: City Lights.

Deleuze, Gilles and Felix Guattari. 1986. *Kafka.* Minneapolis and London: University of Minnesota.

―――. 1977. *Anti-Oedipus.* Trans. Mark Hurley, Mark Seem, and Helen R. Lane. New York: Viking.

Deloria, Jr. Vine. 1991. *Indian Education in America.* Boulder, CO: American Science and Engineering Society.

Delpit, Lisa. 1995. *Other People's Children: Cultural Conflict in the Classroom.* New York: New Press.

Derrida, Jacques. 1974. *Glas.* Paris: Editions Galilee.

De Vise, Daniel. 1997. "Struggling to Bridge the Diversity Gap." *The San Diego Union-Tribune.* 27 July, A1, 14.

Dewey, John. 1915. *Democracy and Education.* New York: Free Press.

Dicker, Susan J. 1996. "Ten Official English Arguments and Counter-Arguments." Official English? No. TESOL's Recommendations for Countering the Official English Movement in the US, TESOL. Online. Altavista. Internet. 31 Jan. 1997. Http://www.ncbe. gwu.edu/miscpubs/tesol/official/arguments.html. Quoting Rosalie Pedalino Porter. 1990. *Forked Tongue: The Politics of Bilingual Education.* New York, Basic Books. n.p.

Dietrich, Deborah, and Kathleen S. Ralph. 1995. "Crossing Borders: Multicultural Literature in the Classroom." *The Journal of Educational Issue of Languages Minority Students* 15 (Winter): n.p. Online. Altavista. Internet. 30 Jan. 1997. Http:// www.gwu.edu/miscpubs/jeilms/vol15/crossing.html. Quoting Toni Morrison. 1992. *Playing in the Dark: Whiteness and the Literary Imagination..* New York: Vintage.

Donagan, Alan. 1988. *Spinoza.* Philosophers in Context Series. 7. New York: Harvester/Wheatsheaf.

Dunbar-Ortiz, Roxanne. 1997. "The Proof of Whiteness: More than Skin Color." Online. Altavista. Internet. 30 Jan.

Dunn, Timothy. 1996. *The Militarization of the U.S.-Mexico Border 1978–1992.* Austin: Center for Mexican American Studies. University of Texas at Austin.

Engel, Diana. 1991. *Gino Badino.* New York: Morrow Junior Books.

Erdrich, Louise. 1988. *Tracks.* Harper & Row.

Evening News, Channel 10, San Diego, 11 October 1996.

Ferry, Luc and Alan Renaut. 1990. *French Philosophy of the Sixties: An Essay on Anti-Humanism.* Trans. Mary H.S. Cattani. Amherst: University of Massachusetts.

Flint, Charley. 1996. "Caring, Sharing, Daring: Reflections on a White Awareness Workshop." *Quarterly Newsletter of the Center for the Study of White American Culture* 2.2: 7–14. Online. Altavista. Internet. 16 Feb. 1997. Http://www.euroamerican. org/articles /caring.html.

Foucault, Michel. 1984. "What is Enlightenment." In *The Foucault Reader*. Ed. Paul Rabinow. New York: Pantheon.

———. 1979. *Discipline and Punish: The Birth of the Prison*. Trans. Alan Sheridan. New York: Vintage.

Fraser, Nancy and Linda Nicholson. 1988. "Social Criticism without Philosophy: An Encounter between Feminism and Postmodernism." *Theory, Culture & Society* 5 no. 2–3:373–4.

Fregoso, Rosa Linda. 1993. *The Bronze Screen: Chicana and Chicano Film Culture*. Minneapolis and London: University of Minnesota.

Freire, Paulo. 1993. *Pedagogy of the City*. New York: Seabury.

———. 1992. *Education for Critical Consciousness*. New York: Continuum.

———. 1990. *Pedagogy of the Oppressed*. New York: Continuum.

Freire, Paulo, and Donaldo Macedo. 1996. "Scientism as a Form of Racism: A Dialogue." In *Measured Lies, The Bell Curve Examined*, ed. Joe L. Kincheloe, Shirley R. Steinberg, and Aaron D. Gresson III. New York: St. Martin's. 423–440.

Gadamer, Hans Georg. 1982. *Truth and Method*. Ed. Garrett Barden and John Cumming. New York: Crossroad Publishing.

Gardner, Howard. 1985. *Frames of Mind: The Theory of Multiple Intelligences*. New York: Basic Books.

Gates, Henry Louis, Jr. 1994. Lecture. Huntington Library. ACLS Curriculum Project.

Ghetto Life 101. National Public Radio. n.d.

Gifted and Talented Program. n.d. San Diego Unified School District.

Gilroy, Paul. 1991. "One Nation under a Groove: The Cultural Politics of 'Race' and Racism in Britain." In *Anatomy of Racism*, ed. David Theo Goldberg. Minneapolis and London: University of Minnesota Press. n.p.

Giroux, Henry. 1991. Border Pedagogy in the Age of Postmodernism. In *Border Pedagogy: Postmodern Education, Politics, Culture and Social Criticism.* Minneapolis and London: University of Minnesota Press. n.p.

Giroux, Henry, and Peter McLaren. 1991. "Leon Golub's Radical Pessimism: Toward a Pedagogy of Representation." *Exposure* 28 no. 12:18–33.

Graff, Gerald. 1979. *Literature against Itself: Literary Ideas in Modern Society.* Chicago: University of Chicago Press.

Gramsci, Antonio. 1992. On Education. In *Selections from The Prison Notebooks.* Ed. and trans. Quintin Hoare and Geoffrey Nowell Smith. New York; International Publishers. n.p.

Grosz, Elizabeth. 1994. *Volatile Bodies: Towards a Theory of Corporeal Feminism.* Bloomington: Indiana University Press.

Grubb, G., Davis, D. Lum, J. Phihal and C. Morgaine. 1991. *The Cunning Hand, the Cultured Mind: Models for Integrating Vocational and Academic Education.* Berkeley, CA: NCRVE.

Gutiérrez, Kris, and Peter McLaren. 1995. "Pedagogies of Dissent and Transformation." In *Critical Multiculturalism.* Westport, CT: Bergin & Garvey. 125–47.

Gutiérrez-Jones, Carl. 1995. *Rethinking the Borderlands: Between Chicano Culture and Legal Discourse.* Latinos in American Society and Culture Series. Berkeley: University of California Press. Quoting John Guillory. 1987. "Canonical and Non-canonical: a Critique of the Current Debate." *English Literary History* 54:483–57.

Habermas, Jurgen. 1995. "Introduction." Pp. 1–28 in *Observations on the Spiritual Situation of the Age.* Trans. Andrew Buchwalter. Cambridge, MA: MIT Press.

———. 1972. *Knowledge and Human Interests.* Trans. Jeremy Shapiro. London: Heinemann.

Hagedorn, Jessica. 1990. *Dogeaters.* New York: Pantheon.

Haraway, Donna. 1991. A Cyborg Manifesto: Science, Technology, and Socialist Feminism in the Late Twentieth Century. In *Simians, Cyborgs and Women: the Reinvention of Nature*. New York: Routledge, Chapman & Hall. n.p.

Hardt, Michael. 1997. E-mail correspondence with author 25 April.

——. 1993. *Gilles Deleuze, an Apprenticeship in Philosophy*. Minneapolis: University of Minnesota Press.

——. 1991. "Translator's Foreword." Pp. xi–xvi. *The Savage Anomaly: The Power of Spinoza's Metaphysics and Politics* by Antonio Negri. Minneapolis: University of Minnesota.

Hardt, Michael, and Antonio Negri. 1994. *Labor of Dionysus: A Critique of the State-Form*. Minneapolis: University of Minnesota.

Heater, Derek. 1990. *Citizenship, The Civic Ideal in World History, Politics and Education*. New York: Longman.

Hegel, G.W.F. 1967. "On Lordship and Bondage." (1807; trans. 1967). *The Phenomenology of Mind*. Trans. J. B. Baillie. New York: Harper and Row. n.p.

Hernández, Gilbert. 1989. *Blood of Palomar*. Seattle: Fantagraphic Books.

Herrnstein, Richard J., and Charles Murray. 1994. *The Bell Curve*. New York: Free Press.

Hicks, D. Emily. 1996. Nietzsche and Performance. Unpublished.

——. 1995. Foucault's Ventriloquism: Can the Subaltern Speak? Unpublished.

——. 1992. "Robo-raza at the Crossroads." 3 *RLA*: 469–74.

——. 1991. *Border Writing: The Multidimensional Text*. Minneapolis: University of Minnesota Press.

——. dir. 1990. "Breakfast with Sta. Frida: Amalia Mesa-Bains." Performed by Rocío Weiss and Amalia Mesa-Bains. Videotaped interview with Rocío Weiss, BAW/TAF, Capp St., San Francisco, 1990.

——. 1988. "Deterritorialization and Border Writing." In *Ethics/Aesthetics. Postmodern Positions*, ed. R. Merrill. Washington, D.C.: Maisonneuve Press. 47–58.

————. 1985. "Epistemology of the Oppressed: A Theoretical Analysis of Work." *The Writing Instructor.* 5 no. 1:19–29.

Huerta, Jorge. 1982. *Chicano Theatre: Themes and Forms.* Ypsilanti, Mich.: Bilingual Review/Press.

Hurley, Robert. 1988. "Preface." Pp. i–iii in *Spinoza,* by Gilles Deleuze. Trans. Robert Hurley. San Francisco: City Lights.

Hwang, David. 1986. *M. Butterfly.* New York: Penguin Group.

Iglesias, Norma. 1991. *Entre yerba, polvo y plomo, lo fronterizo visto por el cine mexicano.* Tijuana: el Colegio de la Frontera Norte.

Ishitsuka, Shoji. 1996. "Modernity and Social Theory from a Paradigmatic Viewpoint in Social Philosophy." *Journal of Toyama University of International Studies* 6:161–185.

Jameson, Fredric. 1986. "Third World Literature in the Era of Multinational Capitalism." *Social Text* 15 (Fall): 65–88.

————. 1981. *The Political Unconscious: Narrative as Socially Symbolic Act.* Ithaca: Cornell UP.

Jenness, Aylette. 1993. *Ven a mi casa.* New York: New Press.

Kent, Noel Jacob. 1996. "The New Campus Racism: What's Going On?" *Thought and Action, The NEA Higher Education Journal.* 12.2:75–87. Quoting Robert Blauner. 1996. "Self-Segregation Should be Accepted," in *Race Relations.* Wesport, Conn.: Greenhaven Press, 216–223.

Kincheloe, Joe. 1993. *Toward a Critical Politics of Teacher Thinking: Mapping the Postmodern.* Critical Studies in Education and Culture Series. Westport, CT: Bergin and Garvey. Quoting Julian Jaynes. 1976. *The Origin of Consciousness in the Breakdown of the Bicameral Mind.* Boston: Houghton Mifflin.

Kincheloe, Joe, and Shirley Steinberg. 1996. "Who Said It Can't Happen Here?" In *Measure Lies, The Bell Curve Examined,* ed. Joe L. Kincheloe, Shirley R. Steinberg and Aaron D. Gresson III. New York: St. Martin's. 3–47.

Kincheloe, Joe, Shirley Steinberg, and Deborah J. Tippins. *The Stigma of Genius: Einstein and Beyond Modern Education.* Durango, CO: Hollowbrook, 1992.

Krashen, Stephen. 1982. *Principles and Practice in Second Language Acquisition*. New York: Pergamon Press.

Kristeva, Julia. 1986. *The Kristeva Reader*. Ed. Toril Moi. New York: Colombia University Press.

Kymlicka, Will. 1995. *Multinational Citizenship: A Liberal Theory of Minority Rights*. Oxford: Clarendon.

Lewis, Glyn. 1972. *Multilingualism in the Soviet Union*. The Hague: Mouton.

Lippard, Lucy. 1990. *Mixed Blessings; New Art in Multicultural America*. New York: Pantheon Books, 1990.

Lomas Garza, Carmen. 1990. *Family Pictures, Cuadros de familia*. San Francisco: Children's Book Press.

Lugg, Catherine A. 1996. "Attacking Affirmative Action: Social Darwinism as Public PRolicy." In *Measured Lies: The Bell Curve Examined*, ed. Joe L. Kincheloe, Shirley R. Steinberg, and Aaron D. Gresson III. New York: St. Martin's. 367–68. Quoting E. P. Cubberly, 1919. *Education in the United States: A Study and Interpretation of American Educational History*. Boston: Houghton Mifflin. Quoting J. Spring. 1994. *The American School 1642–1993*, 3rd ed. New York: McGraw-Hill. Quoting Carl Bringham. n.d. n.p.

Lunt, Karen. 1998. "Chicana Poets: The New Immigrants in American Literature." Master's Thesis. San Diego State University.

Lyotard, Jean-Francois. 1971. *Discours, Figure*. Paris: Klincksieck.

Macedo, Donaldo. 1994. *Literacies of Power*. Boulder and London: Westview Press.

Macedo, Donaldo and Paulo Freire. 1996. "Scientism as a Form of Racism: A Dialogue." *Measured Lies: The Bell Curve Examined*, ed. Joe L. Kincheloe, Shirley R. Steinberg, and Aaron Gresson III. New York: St. Martin's. 423–440.

MacKinnon, Catherine A. 1989. *Toward a Feminist Theory of the State*. Cambridge: Harvard University Press.

Mahfouz, Naguib. 1990. *Palace Walk*. New York: Doubleday.

Martínez, Elizabeth and Ed McCaughan. 1990. "Chicanas and Mexicanas within a Transnational Working Class." In *Between Borders: Essays on Chicana/Mexicana History*, ed. Adelaida Del Castillo. Encino, CA: Floricanto Press. 31–60.

Massumi, Brian. 1993. "Everywhere You Want to Be: Introduction to Fear." *The Politics of Everyday Fear*. Minneapolis: University of Minnesota Press. 3–37.

McLaren, Peter. 1997. *Revolutionary Multiculturalism: Pedagogies of Dissent for the New Millennium*. The Edge: Critical Studies in Educational Theory Series. Boulder, CO: Westview.

————. 1995. *Critical Pedagogy and Predatory Culture*. London: Routledge.

————. 1994. "Critical Pedagogy: Constructing an Arch of Social Dreaming and a Doorway to Hope." In *Sociology of Education in Canada, Critical Perspectives on Theory, Research and Practice*, ed. Loma Erwin and David MacLennan. Toronto: Copp Clark Longman Ltd. 137–160.

————. 1993. "Multiculturalism and Postmodern Critique: Toward a Pedagogy of Resistance and Transformation." In *Between Borders, Pedagogy and the Politics of Cultural Studies*, ed. H. A. Giroux and P. McLaren. New York: Routledge. 192–222.

————. 1992. *"La educación en los bordes del pensamiento moderno." Entrevista con Adriana Puiggros*. Trans. Balbi, Comba and Lothriger. *Propuesta Educativa, Latinamericana de ciencia sociales*. 4 no. 7:78–81.

————. 1989. *Life in Schools*. New York: Longman.

————. 1988. "Critical Pedagogy and the Politics of Literacy." *Harvard Educational Review* 58 no. 2:213–234.

————. 1986. *Schooling as a Ritual Performance: Towards a Political Economy of Educational Symbols and Gestures*. London: Routledge & Kegan Paul.

————. 1985. "Contemporary Ritual Studies: A Post-Turnerian Perspective." *Semiotic Inquiry* 5 no. 1:78–85.

McLaren, Peter and Kris Gutiérrez. 1997. Global Politics and Local Antagonisms: Research and Practice as Dissent and Possibility. *Revolutionary Multiculturalism: Pedagogies of Dissent for the New Millennium.* The Edge: Critical Studies in Educational Theory Series. Boulder, CO: Westview. 192–222.

McLaren, Peter and Rhonda Hammer. 1992. "Media Knowledges, Warrior Citizenry and Postmodern Literacies." *Journal of Urban and Cultural Studies* 2 no. 2:41–64. Quoting Gerbner, George. 1989/90. "Media Literacy: TV vs. Reality." *Adbusters* 1.12: n.p.

Meehan, Elizabeth. 1993. *Citizenship and the European Community.* London: Sage.

Merod, Jim. 1993. Discussion following Lecture/Performance by Emily Hicks. National University Center for Ethnic and Cultural Studies. San Diego. 29 November.

Michie, Elsie. 1996. "White Chimpanzees and Oriental Despots: Racial Stereotypes and Edward Rochester." In critical edition of Charlotte Bronte, *Jane Eyre,* ed. Beth Newman. New York: St. Martin's. 584–98.

Mies, Maria. 1986. *Patriarchy and Accumulation on a World Scale; Women in the International Division of Labor.* London: Zed Books.

Moi, Toril, ed. 1986. *The Kristeva Reader.* New York: Columbia UP.

Moll, L. C. 1992. "Bilingual Classroom Studies and Community Analysis: Some Recent Trends." *Educational Researcher* 21 no. 20:20–24.

Moraga, Cherríe. 1992. *Shadow of a Man Shattering the Myth: Plays by Hispanic Women,* sel. by Denise Chavez, ed. Linda Feyder. Houston, TX: Arte Publico Press.

———. 1983. *Loving in the War Years, lo que nunca pasó por sus labios.* Boston, MA: South End Press.

———. 1983. *Giving up the Ghost.* Albuquerque, NM: West End Press.

Morton, Carlos. 1983. *El jardín.* In *The Many Deaths of Danny Rosales and other Plays.* Houston, TX: Arte Publico Press, 1983.

Natarajan, Nalini. 1994. "Women, Nation, and Narration in *Midnight's Children*." In *Scattered Hegemonies, Postmodernity and Transnational Feminist Practices*, ed. Inderpal Grewal and Caren Kaplan. Minneapolis: University of Minnesota Press. 76–89.

Nava, Gregory, dir. 1983. *El Norte*. Cinecom International/Island Alive. 139 mins.

Negri, Antonio. 1991. *The Savage Anomaly: The Power of Spinoza's Metaphysics and Politics*, trans. Michael Hardt. Minneapolis: University of Minnesota Press.

Nielson, Aldon Lynn. 1988. *Reading Race: White American Poets and the Racial Discourse in the Twentieth Century*. Athens and London: University of Georgia Press. Quoting John Wieners. 1972. *Selected Poems*. New York: Grossman.

Nieto, Sonia. 1996. *Affirming Diversity: the Sociopolitical Context of Multicultural Education*, 2nd ed. White Plains, NY: Longman. Quoting John U. Ogbu. 1986. "The Consequences of the American Caste System." In *The Social Achievement of Minority Children: New Perspectives*, ed. Ulric Neisser. Hillsdale, NJ: Erlbaum. n.p.

Nietzsche, Friedrich. 1979. On Truth and Lies in a Nonmoral Sense. In *Philosophy and Truth: Selections from Nietzsche's Notebooks of the Early 1870s*. Trans. and ed. Daniel Breaseale. 79–97.

Noriega, Chon, ed. 1992. *Chicanos and Film: Representation and Resistance*. Minneapolis: University of Minnesota Press.

Oakes, J. 1985. *Keeping Track: How Schools Structure Inequality*. New Haven, CT: Yale University Press.

Orenstein, Catherine. (January 1995). "Illegal Transnational Labor." *Journal of International Affairs* 48: 601. Online. Electric Library. Internet. 4 July 1997. Http://www3.elibrary.com/id/250/250/getdo . . . Journal_of_International_Affairs&puburl=0.

Parla, JoAnn. 1994. "Educating Teachers for Cultural and Linguistic Diversity: A Model for All Teachers." *New York State Association for Bilingual Education* 9: 1–6. Online. Altavista. Internet. 31 January 1997. Quoting J.A. Banks. 1994. *Stages of Ethnicity in Multicultural Education*, 3rd ed. Boston: Allyn &

Bacon. J. A. Banks and C. McGee-Banks, eds. 1993. *Multicultural Education: Issues and Perspectives*, 2nd ed. Boston: Allyn & Bacon. C. I. Bennett. 1993. *Comprehensive Multicultural Education: Theory and Practice*, 2nd ed. Boston: Allyn & Bacon.

Patemen, Carole. 1988. *Sexual Contract*. London: Basil Blackwell.

Pellicer López, Carlos 1984. *Julieta y sy caja de colores*. Mexico: Fondo de Cultural Economica.

Perkins, D. N. 1995. *Learnable Intelligence: Breaking the IQ Barrier*. New York: Free Press.

Pesquera, Beatriz M. and Denise A. Segura. 1996. "With Quill and Torch: A Chicana Perspective on the American Women's Movement and Feminist Theories." In *Chicanas at the Crossroads: Social, Economic, and Political Change*, ed. David Maciel and Isidro D. Ortiz. Tucson: University of Arizona Press. 231–247.

Pfeiffer, Kathleen. 1996. "Individualism, Success, and American Identity in the Autobiography of an Ex-Colored Man." *African American Review* 30: n.p. Online. Electric Library. Internet. 4 July 1997.Http://www/3.elibrary.com/id/250/250getdo.... &pubname=African_American_Review&puburl=0.

Pratt, May Louise. 1992. *Imperializing Eyes: Travel Writing and Transculturation*. New York: Routledge.

Quiñónes, Naomi. 1996. 2nd ed. "*Ay que María Felix* (or María was no Virgin)." *Chicana Creativity and Criticism*. María Herrera-Sobek, and Helena María Viramontes. University of New Mexico.

Ra'anan, Uri, María Mesner, Keith Armes, and Kate Martin. 1991. *State and Nation in Multi-Ethnic Societies: The Break-up of Multinational States*. Manchester. Manchester UP.

Rebolledo, Tey Diana. 1995. *Women Singing in the Snow: A Cultural Analysis of Chicana Literature*. Tucson: University of Arizona Press.

Radhakrishnan, Ragagopalan. 1996. *Diasporic Mediations*. Minneapolis: University of Minnesota Press.

Rivera, Roberta. 1992. Conference paper. Latin American Studies Association XVII International Congress. Panel moderator: Mary Louise Pratt. Los Angeles, 24–27 September.

Rose, Gillian. 1978. *The Melancholy Science: an Introduction to the Thought of Theodor W. Adorno.* London: Macmillan.

Rouse, Roger. 1989. "*Mexicano, chicano, pocho: la migración mexicana y el espacio social del postmodernismo.*" *Pagina Uno* 31 December.

Ruiz, Nadeen T., Erminda García, and Richard A. Figueroa. n.p. n.d. *The Ole Curriculum Guide.* San Diego Unified School District.

Saldívar, Ramón. 1990. *Chicano Narrative: the Dialectics of Difference.* Madison: University of Wisconsin Press.

San Miguel, Guadalupe. 1996. "Actors Not Victims: Chicanas/os and the Struggle for Educational Equality." *Chicanas/Chicanos at the Crossroads: Social, Economic, and Political Change,* ed. David Maciel and Isidro D. Ortiz. 159–180.

Sánchez, Rosaura. 1977. "Chicano Bilingualism." *New Scholar* 6:209–226.

Saravia Quiroz, Leobardo, ed. 1990. *En la línea de fuego, relatos policiacos de la frontera.* San Angel: Consejo Nacional para la Cultura y las Artes. 9–16.

Seda, Milagros, and Dennis J. Bixler-Márquez. 1994. "The Ecology of a Chicano Student at Risk." *The Journal of Education Issue of Language Minority Students* 13. (Spring): 195–208. Online. Altavista. Internet. 30 January 1997. http.//www.ncbe.gwu.edu/ miscpubs/ jeilms/vol13/ ecolog13.html.

Semali, Ladislaus. 1995. "In the Name of Science and Genetics and of the Bell Curve: White Supremacy in the Schools." In *Measured Lies: the Bell Curve Examined,* ed. Joe L. Kincheloe, Shirley R. Steinberg and Aaron D. Gresson III. New York: St. Martin's Press. 137–160. Immanuel Wallerstein. 1990. "Culture as the Ideological Battleground of the Modern World System." In *Global Culture, Nationalism, Globalization and Modernity,* ed. M. Featherstone. Beverly Hills, CA: Sage. n.p.

Shelton, Allen. 1996. "The Ape's IQ." *Measured Lies: the Bell Curve Examined*, ed. Joe L. Kincheloe, Shirley R. Steinberg, and Aaron D. Gresson III. New York: St. Martin's Press. 91–105.

Soto, Gary. 1996. "Mexican Begin Jogging." *Literature, Reading and Responding to Fiction, Poetry, Drama and the Essay*, ed. Joel Wingard. New York: HarperCollins. 782.

Spinner, Jeff. 1994. *The Boundaries of Citizenship, Race, Ethnicity, and Nationality in the Liberal State*. Baltimore and London: Johns Hopkins University Press. Quoting Rorty. n.d. n.p

Spinoza, Baruch. 1992. *Ethics, Treatise on the Emendation of the Intellect and Selected Letters*. Ed. Seymour Feldman. Trans. Samuel Shirley. Indianapolis and Cambridge: Hackett Publishing Co.

Spivak, Gayatri. 1988. "Can the Subaltern Speak?" *Marxism and the Interpretation of Culture*, ed. Cary Nelson and Lawrence Grossberg. Urbana and Chicago: University of Illinois Press. 271–313.

———. 1993. "Woman in Difference." *Outside in the Teaching Machine*. New York. Routledge. 77–95.

Swisher, Karen. 1994. "American Indian Learning Styles Survey: An Assessment of Teacher's Knowledge." *The Journal of Education Issues of Language Minority Students* 13 (Spring): 59–77. Online. Electric Library. Internet. 31 Jan. 1997. Http:// www.ncbe.gwu.edu /miscpubs/ jeilms/vol13/americ13.html.

Trembath, Paul. 1996. "Aesthetics Without Art or Culture: Toward an Alternative Sense of Materialist Agency." *Strategies* 9/10:122–51.

Turner, Bryan. 1992. "Prolegomena to a General Theory of the Social Order." *Proceedings of Seminars on Citizenship organized by the Economic and Social Research Council*, ed. Bryan Turner. Swindon: ESRC. n.p.

———. 1986. *Citizenship and Capitalism. The Debate over Reformism*. London: Allen and Unwin.

Viramontes, Helena. 1996. "Miss Clairol." 2nd ed. *Chicana Creativity and Criticism*, ed. María Herrera-Sobek and H. Viramontes. Albuquerque: University of New Mexico. 164–168.

Viswanathan, Gauri. 1989. *Masks of Conquest: Literary Study and British Rule in India*. New York: Columbia University Press.

Walkowitz, Daniel. 1994. "Reviews: The Wages of Whiteness: Race and the Making of the American Working Class, by David R. Roediger." *Journal of American Ethnic History* 14 (Sept. 1): 98. Online. Electric Library. Internet. 4 July 1997. Http:// www.3.elibrary.com/id/250/250/getdo.journal_of_ American_Ethnic_History&puburl=0.

Wallace, Amy. 1996. "Less Diversity Seen as UC Preferences End." *Los Angeles Times*. 2 October. A1, 18.

Wallerstein, Immanuel. 1974. *The Modern World System*. New York: Academic Press.

Walters, Ronald. 1997. "Race in America: Multiculturalism, Afrocentrism, and the New Democratic Framework." *The Black Collegian* 26 (1996): 32(4). Online. Electric Library. Internet. 4 July 1997. Http:// www3.elibrary.com/id/50/250/getdo . . . m=RL&pubname=The_Black_collegian&puburl=0.

Ware, Vron. 1997. "Moments of Danger: Race, Gender, and Memories of an Empire." Abstract. *History & Theory*. Online. Electric Library. Internet. (3 July) Http://www3.elibrary. com.id250/ 250/getdo. . . rm=RL&pubname=History_˜A˜_Theory&puburl=0.

Warren, S. 1984. *The Emergence of Dialectical Theory*. Chicago: University of Chicago Press.

West, Cornel. 1992. "Diverse New World." In *Debating P.C.: The Controversy over Political Correctness on College Campuses*. ed. P. Berman. New York: Laurel/Bantam Doubleday Dell. 326–332.

Willis, Paul. 1977. *Learning to Labour: How Working Class Kids Get Working Class Jobs*. Aldershot, England: Gower.

Winant, Howard. 1997. "Behind Blue Eyes: Contemporary White Racial Politics." Online. Altavista. Internet. (16 February) Http:/ /blue. temple.edu/˜winant/whitness.html. Quoting David R. Roediger. 1991. *The Wages of Whiteness: Race and the Making of the American Working Class*. New York: Verso.

Wynter, Sylvia. 1979. "Sambos and Minstrels." *Social Text, Theory, Culture, Ideology* 1 no. 1:149–156. Quoting Gilles Deleuze and Felix Guattari. n.d. n. p.

Yarbro-Bejarano, Yvonne. 1990. "The Female Subject in Chicana Theatre: Sexuality, 'Race,' and Class." *Performing Feminisms: Feminist Critical Theory and Theatre*, ed. Sue-Ellen Case. Baltimore, MD: Johns Hopkins University Press. 131–49.

Zuñiga, Carmen, and Sylvia Alatorre Alva. 1995. "Parents as Resources in Schools: A Community-of-Learners Perspective." *Journal of Education Issues of Language Minority Students* 16.13: n.p. Online. Altavista. Internet. 30 January 1997. Http.//www.ncbe. gwu. edu/ miscpubs/jeilms/vl 16/jeilms1613.html.

Index

Index 181

Studies in the Postmodern Theory of Education

General Editors
Joe L. Kincheloe & Shirley R. Steinberg

Counterpoints publishes the most compelling and imaginative books being written in education today. Grounded on the theoretical advances in criticalism, feminism and postmodernism in the last two decades of the twentieth century, Counterpoints engages the meaning of these innovations in various forms of educational expression. Committed to the proposition that theoretical literature should be accessible to a variety of audiences, the series insists that its authors avoid esoteric and jargonistic languages that transform educational scholarship into an elite discourse for the initiated. Scholarly work matters only to the degree it affects consciousness and practice at multiple sites. Counterpoints' editorial policy is based on these principles and the ability of scholars to break new ground, to open new conversations, to go where educators have never gone before.

For additional information about this series or for the submission of manuscripts, please contact:

Joe L. Kincheloe & Shirley R. Steinberg
637 West Foster Avenue
State College, PA 16801